JAPANESE MANAGEMENT OVERSEAS

JAPANESE MANAGEMENT OVERSEAS

Experiences In The United States And Thailand

by HIROSHI KOMAI

1989 ASIAN PRODUCTIVITY ORGANIZATION TOKYO

Some other titles published by the Asian Productivity Organization:

— *The Japanese Firm in Transition*
— *Japanese Management: A Forward Looking Analysis*
— *Japanese-Style Management: Its Foundations and Prospects*
— *Management by Objectives: A Japanese Experience*
— *Company-Wide Total Quality Control*
— *Introduction to Quality Engineering: Designing Quality into Products and Processes*
— *Guide to Quality Control*
— *Quality Control Circles at Work*
— *Japan's Quality Control Circle*
— *100 Management Charts*
— *Modern Production Management: A Japanese Experience*
— *Profitability Analysis: Japanese Approach*

Designed and Printed in Hong Kong by
NORDICA INTERNATIONAL LIMITED
for
Asian Productivity Organization
4-14, Akasaka 8-chome
Minato-ku, Tokyo 107, Japan

© Asian Productivity Organization 1989

ISBN: 92-833-1101-9 (Casebound)
ISBN: 92-833-1102-7 (Limpbound)

Preface

Modern industrial society's structures and institutions have evolved to the point where they oppress the human spirit in a number of ways. This is most apparent in industrial labor. With industry relying on mass production, today's workers are stripped of their creativity and pride of work. Day after day, they toil at monotonous, repetitive tasks devoid of any personal meaning.

This trend is especially evident in Japan. Japan has today become one of the largest industrial powers in the world, and Japanese management is looked up to worldwide. Yet the Japanese management philosophy is one of emphasizing productivity above all else — what might be called a philosophy of productivitism. Even though it may pay token homage to the peripheral trappings of humanizing the workplace, it is inherently incompatible with this humanization. Labor unions, which might be expected to represent the workers' interests and to check this over-emphasis on productivity, have instead been equally materialistic in settling for monetary rewards and tacitly approving management's blatant disregard for the quality of the worker's life. Even the workers themselves, fearing unemployment and preoccupied with money to satisfy their craving for security, have had little time to worry about the root problem of dehumanized labor.

In most cases, one would expect such dehumanizing conditions to also be demoralizing and hence counterproductive. Yet Japanese management somehow managed to maintain a high level of productivity. Although much has been written on Japanese management, there has been very little on this accomplishment. It is my aim in this book to draw upon empirical data from field research to explain how Japanese management has managed to square this circle.

Another reason for writing this book is that I want to encourage other writers in international sociology. International economics and international politics are already firmly established disciplines in their own right, but we seldom even hear the term international sociology. Nevertheless, there is broad agreement on the need for international sociology to study the impact of contact between and among different cultures. Thus I hope to provide an example of such intercultural contact by examining the transplantability of Japanese management to non-Japanese environments.

The data in this book has been gathered from various surveys conducted over the last 10 years. I began this by concentrating on Southeast Asia, especially Thailand, and then teamed up with Mr. Mitsuhiko Yamada, a respected sociologist who is also a Nikko Research Center director, in a joint research effort that generated much of the comparative data on Japanese management in Southeast Asia, America, and Japan. Although much of this work has already been published, this book is not a rehash of these previous papers. Instead I have completely rewritten the material to incorporate new insights.

In my previous papers, I had emphasized the conditions for and impact of transplanting Japanese management into a foreign culture, assuming that the desire for high productivity would naturally entail a high level of worker satisfaction. In short, I had accepted the prevailing theory. However, this theory refused to jibe with the data. For one thing, it left unexplained the fact that Japanese workers were more able than American workers to maintain simultaneously a high level of productivity and a low level of satsifaction. If it is satisfaction that leads to high productivity, as the traditional theory argues, this combination should be unsustainable. While I was still in the conceptual stage of my writing, it occurred to me that productivity and the humanization of work are two entirely distinct dimensions, that the possibility of self-actualization is at the heart of humanizing work, and that the whole thrust of this book must be dedicated to trying to resolve this paradox. Thus I had to completely rewrite the material to reflect this new concept. However, once it became clear what the basic structure was, data that had previously seemed contradictory now made sense. This was an especially satisfying experience.

There are admittedly many limitations in the attitude surveys in this book. Were the questions asked really the best? Were the sample sizes adequate? Was I right to measure productivity not as demonstrated in hard numbers but rather as represented in worker attitudes? Yet despite these questions, I believe this book is valuable for its very clean approach and its consistent explanation.

Given the worldwide economic slump and the yen's dramatic appreciation, Jananese industry has increasingly had to locate more and more of its production facilities overseas. And if Japanese management is revised to better accommodate foreign cultures and its non-universal aspects removed, it should be transplantable along with Japanese industry. As noted in this book, Japanese management has been effective in mitigating the worker's sense of alienation and increasing productivity. But it is worth remembering that there has been no real humanization of work and that productivitism is the byword in Japan, birthplace of Japanese management.

As a scholar and writer, I intend to continue my effort to identify the limitations of industrial society and to discover an alternative social order that would be free of these limitations. Despite the difficulties of the task, I feel a solution is possible.

I would like to express my heartfelt appreciation to all of the people who made the publication of this book possible. While they cannot all be mentioned, there are a few who deserve to be singled out. First of all, I would like to thank all of the workers in America, Thailand, and Japan who took the time to answer the survey questions as well as their companies for allowing me to do the surveys. At the same time, I owe a special debt of gratitude to my mentor, Dr. Kunio Odaka, who not only gave me invaluable scholarly advice on numerous occasions but also introduced me to the Asian Productivity Organization and made the publication of this book possible in English. And last but certainly not least, special thanks go to the translator, Mr. Fred Uleman, as well as to Ms. Yukiko Katayama and Mr. Nazim Zaidi at the APO for shepherding this text through to publication.

Hiroshi Komai

Matsudo (Japan), December 1988

Contents

Chapter 1

The Japanese Management Boom

The Crisis in American Management

There has been a crisis in American management since the late 1970s. This crisis has been most pronounced in the automobile industry, the prototype American industry, as Japanese automakers have made steady inroads into the American market. Although many reasons have been cited for this Japanese success, there is no doubt that the decline in American labor morale, and hence the decline in American productivity, has been a major cause.

This was most strikingly demonstrated by the events at Lordstown. The Lordstown (Ohio) plant was supposed to be the jewel in GM's crown. It boasted highly automated production using the most modern facilities, but it was shut down in 1972 by a walkout protesting the line speed and the robot-like work. In many ways, this walkout was a rebellion against technology-centered management.[1] Nor was Lordstown an isolated case. The same pattern was later repeated at Ford's Mahwah (New Jersey) Plant. At this plant, people on the "graveyard" shift found their work so dull that they resorted to smoking marijuana, frequent and unauthorized absenteeism, and general thievery to relieve the tedium. Eventually, productivity and quality deteriorated to the point that the plant had to be closed in 1980.[2]

In all of these cases — and there were many more — it was found that the high labor mobility, rampant absenteeism, thievery, walkouts, and wanton destruction of company property were triggered by the increasingly dehumanized nature of the work.

Working in an auto plant is a very impersonal experience. John F. Runcie, a scholar who spent five months working on an auto assembly line, found the repetition and boredom almost unbearable. The only ways to escape this tedium were either to call in sick or to devise ways to fight it in the plant. Among the most commonly employed means were shutting your mind to your surroundings, talking with other people, playing games, and even trading jobs. When these did not work, people turned to drink, drugs, sabotage, and vandalism.[3]

Although the essential tedium and repetition of work remains unchanged, there is a change underway in the quality of workers and their thinking. According to Daniel Yankelovich, American values are undergoing a rapid change. Getting ahead and making more money are no longer the motivating forces they once were, and people are now motivated by the instrinsic rewards they gain from the work itself.[4] It is only natural that these new values clash with today's increasingly repetitive work and authoritarian workplaces. According to a study by the University of Michigan's Survey Research Center, American workers have become increasingly dissatisfied with their work, by any measure, throughout the 1970s.[5]

It was against this background that American business became interested in Japanese management. The need to rebuild American industry was eloquently argued by Amitai Etzioni in 1979, who pointed out how Japanese management could contribute to this reindustrialization. The mass media have greatly jumped on this bandwagon.

Business Week, for example, ran a cover-story feature on this theme in 1980 under the title "A New Social Contract." In what turned out to be one of the most-commented-on features that *Business Week* has ever run, *Business Week* emphasized the need to learn from Japan in encouraging teamwork at all levels and advocated the adoption of the Japanese practice of quality control (QC) circles. The broadcast media have also done their part. In 1980, NBC broadcast a special entitled *If Japan Can, Why Can't We?* that, contrasting the sick state of American industry with the vigor in Japan, conveyed a message of Japanese managerial superiority and achieved very high ratings and considerable post-showing comment nationwide.

Summing up this swelling tide, Worldwatch's Bruce Stokes wrote in "East Teaches West: Reaping Profits from Worker Participation in Management"[6] and again in "The Japanese May Provide Aid to Ailing U.S. Industries"[7] of the need for a "Japanese Marshall Plan for American industry." This infatuation with Japanese management was also supported by generally positive feelings about Japan itself. Edwin O. Reischauer's *The Japanese*[8] and Ezra F. Vogel's *Japan As Number One*[9] were widely read in the United States. These Japanologists' ideas were given further credence and theoretical structure by George C. Lodge's advocacy of communitarianism.

Believing that the United States had much to learn from Japan, a nation that had succeeded with both industrialization and democratization, Lodge suggested a new ideology for American based upon what he perceived as the Japanese ideology. Intended to supplant the emerging American ideology, this was defined as the synthesis of five prime elements: (i) communitarianism (making the community central) in place of individualism, and with it a new emphasis on consensus instead of contracts and on adapting to inequality instead of make-believe equality, (ii) membership rights in place of property rights, (iii) decision-making based upon the needs of the community instead of on competitive principles, (iv) the state as planner rather than the limited state, and (v) holism in place of scientific specialization.[10]

Can Japanese management meet these American expectations? Before attempting to answer this question, it is important first to look at American management itself and to analyze it to see how it is structured and what the basic managerial principles are. Only then can we meaningfully see if Japanese management provides a possible remedy for its ills.

American Managerial Concepts

Although the humanization of work should be a basic concern of modern management, it has traditionally been neglected in favor of productivity. Relegated to secondary status at best, the humanization of work has never been integrated into productivity theories. As a result, people have generally looked at humanizing the work only in terms of what it can contribute to higher productivity, and the two concepts have been viewed as going hand in hand. However, they exist independent of each other; and there are times when they are in convergence and times when they are in conflict.

Figure 1-1 shows how the leading American management theorists have percieved the relationship between humanization and productivity. As seen, the horizontal axis indicates the degree of emphasis on humanizing the work (with increasing humanization moving to the right) and the vertical axis indicates the emphasis on productivity (with higher productivity toward the top). In the first quadrant there is a strong drive for both humanized work and high productivity, in the second quadrant there is a strong drive for high productivity but little concern for humanizing work, in the third quadrant there is little desire for either productivity or humanization, and in the fourth quadrant the drive is for humanization of work but low productivity.

Perhaps the first major focus of American management theory was Frederick W. Taylor's scientific management, shown in Figure 1-1 in the second quadrant. Scientific management entailed having experts do time-and-motion studies, breaking all of the work down into its constituent elements and measuring the time required for each element to scientifically discover the best methods and best tools for doing the work.[11] It was Henry Ford's genius to see how this could be applied to the modern assembly line.

Taylor believed that maximum prosperity could be achieved for both employer and employee by maximizing labor productivity, and he thus advocated a mental revolution for employees and employers alike.[12] Attempting to introduce scientific management without providing higher wages and other employee rewards would, he argued, alienate the workers and invite militancy.[13] Aware of the problems created by the increasing routinization of work, Taylor believed that they could be solved by enabling workers to learn new skills and to move on to increasingly complex and sophisticated tasks.[14]

Reinhard Bendix has explained the circumstances leading to the emergence of this management ideology as follows. Prior to Taylor, management had lorded over the workers in a kind of social darwinism. The rise of trade unionism led management to demand that it be granted absolute authority and greater obedience. Questioning management's claim to better judgment and superior abilities, Taylor sought to control production scientifically.[15] It might be added that this approach succeeded with the tacit approval of the unions, which emphasized the external rewards and did not pay much attention to the content of the work itself.

Whatever its theoretical underpinnings, it is clear that the drive for ever-greater productivity and the willingness to reward productive workers with higher wages lead unerringly to the dehumanization of work. In the process, work became the most routine of rote tasks and each worker was assigned a simple, standardized skill. One of the core concepts in this approach was the idea of the interchangability of labor. Taylor stressed that workers should not be lumped together but should be treated as discrete individuals.[16] Since the work was standardized and broken down into simple units, it did not matter who did any specific task and it was very easy to replace one worker with another. In effect, this was the attainment of what Frederick Herzberg has termed, "interchangeable people working on the interchangeable parts of the interchangeable assembly line."[17]

Productivity enhancement was also the underlying value for the theorists who followed Taylor. Among them, Elton Mayo and his theory of human relations, Chris Argyris and his critique of the organization, and Rensis Likert and his managerial system theory were especially influential. Like Taylor, Mayo was interested in productivity and restrictions on output, and he finally decided that human factors were decisive. To summarize the two most important findings to come out of studies conducted by Mayo and his associates at Western Electric's Hawthorne plant outside of Chicago, (i) the output of female workers in the test room rose slowly to stabilize at a record high, but this was completely unrelated to experimental changes in the physical working conditions and was rather the result of the fact that the atmosphere within the test room did not have the same constraints and feelings of personal futility that existed outside the test room[18] and

(ii) there were informal organizations in the room and workers, seeking to preserve their position by obeying the group conduct norms, restricted output even when this was counter to their own economic interests.[19] And where these restrictions on output existed, there was a conflict between loyalty to the company and loyalty to co-workers.

Thus the Hawthorne study team suggested a counseling program for improved two-way communication between the company and workers as one practical means of helping the individual to adjust and to implement changes.[20] This later came to be called the human relations approach.

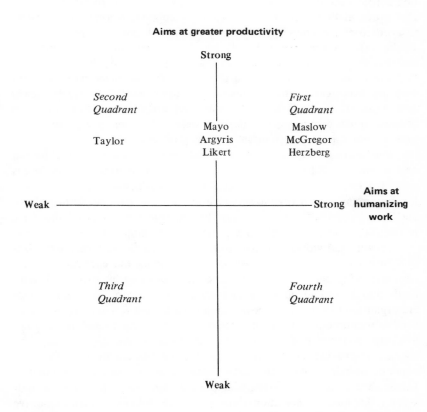

Figure 1-1. Conflict between Productivity and Humanization of Work

According to Mayo himself, the problem is not simply one of restricting output but is the lack of communication and the feelings of futility that led to the restrictions on productivity.[21] In this sense, it signals an awareness of the worker as a cooperator whose personality and attitudes must be respected within the organization.[22] Despite this, the human relations approach was unable to correct the basic causes of the restrictions on output and sought to paper over the situation with deceptive attitudinal manipulation, with the result that it was rightly criticized for not ultimately leading to any significant increase in production.

Argyris found that the basic incongruence between the mature personality and the formal organization resulted in low worker identification with the company and hence low productivity. While the formal organization is composed of task specialization and a chain of command in a hierarchal order, if these principles were ideally applied, workers would work in an environment where: (i) they exercise minimal control over the workday world, (ii) they are expected to be passive, dependent, and subordinate, (iii) they are expected to have a short time perspective, (iv) they are induced to perfect and value the frequent use of a few superficial skills, and (v) they are expected to produce under conditions leading to psychological failure. In effect, "All these characteristics are incongruent to the ones healthy human beings are postulated to desire. They are much more congruent with the needs of infants in our culture."

This incongruence between the mature personality and the formal organization would thus inevitably increase (i) the more mature the employees are, (ii) the more clear-cut and logically tight the formal structure is made for maximum formal organizational effectiveness, (iii) the further down the line of command one goes, and (iv) the more mechanized the work is (i.e., the more assembly-line principles are employed).[23]

Thus the individual can adapt to this conflict with the formal organization by (i) leaving the organization, (ii) climbing the corporate ladder, (iii) employing defense mechanisms, or (iv) lowering his own work standards and becoming apathetic and disinterested. Informal work groups are organized to perpetuate these individual adaptive acts and provide feedback to reinforce individual attitudes, resulting in output restrictions, goldbricking, and group slowdowns.[24]

Likert provided an answer to the questions posed by Argyris. As a result of his studies of the functional characteristics of management control, Likert showed that there were four possible systems. Naming these four systems for their organizational characteristics, he called them exploitive authoritative, benevolent authoritative, consultative, and participative.[25] He also found that both productivity and worker morale decline the closer management approximates the exploitive authoritative mode and increase the closer it approximates the group participative mode.[26]

There are three basic concepts underlying the participation group system of management. First is the principle of supportive relations by which the individual in the organization feels supported by the interpersonal relations and interworkings of the organization and maintains a sense of personal worth and importance. Second is the principle of group decision making within the multiple, overlapping group structure. This is not the traditional man-to-man model of interaction (i.e., superior to subordinate), but is one in which decisions are made by the group in an overlapping structure with each group linked to other groups. As a result, the organization here is not the traditional line organization or even the line/staff organization but is a complex grid structure. The third principle is that of having the employees themselves set and aspire to high performance targets.[27]

The reason that participation group management in line with these three principles results in high morale and high productivity is because workers have favorable attitudes toward their superiors, communication is good, and there is a strong sense of peer-group loyalty. Peer leadership is especially important, since it can work to increase output as well as to restrict it[28]

While there was increasing emphasis on the humanization of work as theory moved from Taylor to Mayo, Argyris, and Likert, this was primarily a realization that ignoring the human dimensions of work resulted in lower productivity. The humanization of work was not a primary concern for these theorists, with enhanced productivity remaining their ultimate goal. Thus they may be characterized as very concerned with increasing productivity and indifferent to the human dimensions of the work *per se*, putting them between the first and second quadrants on Figure 1-1.

Independent of Taylor's scientific management and the discovery of human factors, A. H. Maslow's self-actualization theory has had an increasing influence on modern management. Maslow's theory of self-actualization is fundamentally different from Taylor's scientific management in that it says higher productivity naturally results from the humanization of work. As Maslow explains it, proper management is not "simply in terms of improved production, improved quality control, improved labor relations, [and] improved management of creative personnel" but is management that "can improve the people involved and improve the world."[29]

According to Maslow's theory of the human personality, human needs may be ranked on a hierarchy from the lowest basic physical needs to the highest need for self-actualization. So long as the lower needs are not satisfied, the higher needs do not make themselves felt. Yet once the lower needs are satisfied, the higher needs come into play. From bottom to top, these needs are for physiological sustenance, for safety, for belonging and love, for esteem, and for self-actualization. The physiological and safety needs are self-evident. The need for belonging and love is essentially a desire for affectionate relationships in general and for a place in the group or family. The need for esteem is a need for self-esteem, self-respect, and the esteem of others. And the need for self-actualization is the individual's need to realize his potential. It is the desire to be all that he possibly can. It should be repeated, however, that this need for self-actualization does not emerge unless the lower needs (physiological needs, safety, love, and esteem) have already been met.[30]

Seen from the present, Maslow's hierarchy of needs may also be termed a ranking of the ease with which the different needs can be satiated. Because the lower needs are most easily met, meeting them soon ceases to be an immediate concern. By contrast, the higher needs are difficult to satisfy and hence continue to be important to the individual. Thus it may be postulated that all of these needs exist simultaneously and in parallel.

Whatever the theoretical details, it is clear that the best management is that management that facilitates self-actualization, and that such management will also result in higher productivity. Thus Maslow has been placed in the first quadrant in Figure 1-1 because of his strong emphasis on both the humanization of work and the achievement of high productivity. In turn, Maslow's theory of self-actualization gave birth to Douglas McGregor's Theory Y and Herzberg's theory of motivation/hygiene factors. Both of these men are in basic agreement with Maslow in arguing that the humanization of work is prerequisite to productivity gains.

Looking first at McGregor's Theory Y, McGregor has postulated that there are basically two diametrically opposing ways of treating people. One is the traditional theory with its emphasis on directions and control. This he calls Theory X, and it is premised upon the assumptions that (i) people have an inherent dislike of work, (ii) they therefore must be coerced, controlled, directed, and threatened with punishment, and (iii) people actually prefer to be controlled, wish to avoid responsibility, have relatively little ambition, and want security above all. People managed in accord with this theory see work as a kind of punishment and as the price to be paid for the many pleasures they can obtain outside the job.

In contrast to this traditional position, McGregor says there is also a pattern that seeks to integrate individual goals (self-actualization) and organizational goals (productivity). This he calls Theory Y. Theory Y is premised upon the assumptions that: (i) depending upon controllable conditions, work may be a source of satisfaction or a source of punishment, (ii) man will exercise self-direction and self-control in the service of objectives to which he is committed, (iii) commitment to objectives is a function of the rewards, e.g., the satisfaction of ego and self-actualization needs,

(iv) people learn, under proper conditions, not only to accept but to seek responsibility, (v) the capacity to exercise a relatively high degree of imagination, ingenuity, and creativity in the solution of organizational problems is widely, not narrowly, distributed in the population, and (vi) under the conditions of modern industrial life, the average person's intellectual potential is only being partially utilized.[31]

In sum, the central tenet of Theory X is that of the hierarchy with clear exercise of authority through command and control, while Theory Y is based upon the integration of individual and corporate goals.

While Theory Y uses the concept of self-driven behavior, McGregor employs basically the same hierarchy of human needs as postulated by Maslow. Starting from the lowest, these are physiological needs, the need for safety, social needs, personal needs, and self-actualization.[32] The idea of social needs as used by McGregor is basically the same as Maslow's need for belonging and love, and the personal needs roughly the same as Maslow's need for recognition.

Next is Herzberg's theory of motivation/hygiene factors. In this, Herzberg argues that the factors producing job satisfaction are separate and distinct from the factors creating job dissatisfaction. Job satisfaction factors include achievement, recognition, the job itself, responsibility, and the potential for promotion and growth. Yet while the presence of these factors can result in satisfaction, their absence seldom results in dissatisfaction. Of them, the job itself, responsibility, and promotions are long-term satisfaction factors, and recognition is in the sense of recognition for achievement. By contrast, job dissatisfaction is determined by company policies and management, supervision, wages, interpersonal relations, working conditions, status, job security, and the impact on the individual's private life. All of the dissatisfactions generated by these factors are short-term. Just as the absence of satisfaction factors does not generate dissatisfaction, the absence of dissatisfaction factors is not easily translatable into satisfaction. Because the dissatisfaction factors essentially describe the work environment and serve primarily to prevent job dissatisfaction, they have been termed hygiene factors. The satisfaction factors, on the other hand, because they motivate the individual to superior performance and effort, have been termed motivators.[33] It is the motivators that compel people to stay with a given organization, and the hygiene factors that propel them to leave it.[34]

As may be seen, the hygiene factors roughly correspond to Maslow's lower needs and the motivators to the higher needs. The hygiene factors, like the lower needs, are easily satiated, such that just as they lose their power as rewards and incentives, they take on added force as deterrents and disincentives.[35] Particularly noteworthy is that Herzberg had found that these motivators correlate positively, and the hygiene factors negative-ly, with productivity, job performance and morale. This means that both morale and productivity improve when management is oriented toward self-actualization, and this is in agreement with McGregor's contention. As a result, McGregor and Herzberg have been placed in the first quadrant of Figure 1-1 indicating that they emphasize both productivity and the humanization of work.

Although everyone since Taylor has continued to make production a general goal, the trend has been increasingly to emphasize the importance of the human factors of work. In recent years, this trend has given rise to a new concern with the quality of work life, which is the subject of the next section.

Quality of Work Life

It was the 1972 *Work in America* report of the Special Task Force to the Secretary of Health, Education, and Welfare that forcibly impressed upon the American consciousness the need to recognize that the pursuit of humanizing work is separate from the pursuit of production and em-phatically emphasized the need to improve the quality of work life (QWL).[36] This report notes explicitly that QWL is directed not at im-proved production efficiency but at social efficiency. Through enhancing QWL, society can avoid "some of the very large costs of such job-related pathologies as political alienation, violent aggression against others, alcoholism and drug abuse, mental depression, an assortment of physical illnesses, inadequate performance in schools, and a larger number of welfare families than there need be. These costs are borne by the citizen and by society."[37]

While this report thus took a social cost-benefit approach to promoting QWL, the international trend is toward making the humanization of work itself the objective. One of the most famous examples is the white paper issued by the Commission of the European Community in 1973 calling for a number of reforms, including an effort to eliminate assembly line work from plants throughout the EC. Another is the 1975 resolution by the International Labour Organisation (ILO) on making work more human.

According to Ted Mills, one of the leaders of the QWL movement in the United States, while industrial democracy is being established in Europe as a means of humanizing work, Americans have adopted the QWL idea.[38] While there is a transfer of authority from the capitalist owners to the laborers and unions in Europe consistent with Europe's socialist traditions, the American tradition is more individualistic and resentful of government control.

How is QWL defined? Richard E. Walton, a leading authority on QWL, although he uses the term "work innovation" in preference to

10

the term QWL, cites the following nine points as characterizing QWL: (i) autonomous work groups and self-management, (ii) integrated support functions free of staff functions and job specialization, (iii) challenging job assignments, (iv) job mobility and rewards for learning, (v) facilitative leadership, (vi) managerial decision information for operators, (vii) self-government for the plant community, (viii) congruent physical and social context, and (ix) learning and evolution.[39]

Likewise, Jerome M. Rosow of the Work in America Institute cites the following ten factors in improving QWL: (i) full and fair wages, (ii) fringe benefits, (iii) a safe and healthful work environment, (iv) job security, (v) free collective bargaining, (vi) growth and progress (a personnel system that sees employees as resources for growth and progress), (vii) social unity (creation of a work environment that workers can identify with and where they can feel that the work they are doing is important, with special emphasis on teamwork and cooperation work), (viii) participation, (ix) industrial democracy, and (x) concern for the total life (concern for harmony between work and worker's lifestyle).[40]

However, when these various lists are examined, it seems that QWL is essentially a question of (i) redesigning the workplace, (ii) participative management, and (iii) self-management of group activities.

The redesign of the workplace is an attempt to redesign the work so that it more closely facilitates self-actualization. Argyris has proposed doing this with job enlargement, increasing the number of tasks performed by the employee along the flow of work.[41] Herzberg, contending that there is no point in simply collecting meaningless fragments together, has rejected job enlargement in favor of job enrichment, and has argued that what is needed is not horizontal enlargement but vertical enrichment. The eight elements that he postulates for job enrichment are: (i) direct feedback from the results of behavior, (ii) client relationship, (iii) new learning, (iv) scheduling, (v) unique expertise, (vi) control over resources, (vii) direct communication authority, and (viii) personal accountability.[42] In addition, redesigning the work includes job rotations.

As defined by Kunio Odaka, participative management is a concept including participation in decision-making at each corporate level and at each stage of the production process. In this concept, Odaka sees both industrial democracy with labour representatives participating in the organization's decision-making and self-managed group activities as will be discussed below as elements of participative management.[43]

The European experience is very instructive on industrial democracy. Of the many experiments that have been tried, particular attention has been paid first to the establishment of an active organization of plant employees (not the labor union) and having employee representatives participate in

11

board meetings. This system was legally mandated in France in 1946 and in West Germany in 1952.[44] In the 1970s, legalization spread to the Scandinavian countries and other countries throughout Europe. The second point of particular attention is self-management at the plant level. This was systematically introduced in Yugoslavia in 1950 and has since spread throughout Eastern Europe.[45]

Self-management of work groups derives from the idea that workers have the right of self-determination and self-management in the workplace.[46] Argyris has proposed the formation of individual-need-oriented groups separate from the formal organization.[47] The British idea of socio-technical systems is close to this concept.[48] In addition, this movement is also supported by the East European trend toward self-management.

Among the best-known examples of companies that have actually instituted QWL programs are two automakers: Volvo of Sweden and GM of the United States. Volvo president Pehr G. Gyllenhammar has summarized Volvo's innovation in pursuit of the humanization of work as follows. "The ideal goal for the new plan was to make it possible for an employee to see a blue Volvo driving down the street and say to himself: I made that car."[49] The innovation at the Kalmar plant involved both doing away with the assembly line and forming autonomous human groups. In place of the line, Volvo introduced individual carriers (electrically powered platforms capable of carrying a single vehicle) controlled by the workers. The second focus, the autonomous human working groups, were groups of approximately 20 workers voluntarily taking joint responsibility for their work. Inspection stations were eliminated. The only contract the workers had with management was to make a certain number of vehicles.

It is noteworthy here that, as a result of these innovations, Volvo achieved striking improvements in morale (low morale having previously shown up in high employee turnover, absenteeism, wildcat strikes, and other problems) and improved productivity. Although the Kalmar plant was somewhat more expensive to build than other plants, the improved productivity more than offset these added costs.[50]

In Volvo's Torslanda plant, the revolution manifested itself in (i) the establishment of a hierarchy of work councils, (ii) job enhancement, and (iii) expanded autonomy in group working. The work councils include representatives from both labor and management. For job enhancement, the company initially introduced job rotations every day or half-day and later gave the workers themselves the authority to conduct inspections and to decide whether or not reworking was needed. With autonomy, production requirements rested on the group, not on the individual, with the result that all of the work became group work. Here too, there was a dramatic improvement in morale and sharply improved product quality.

One of the lessons learned from this plant was that there is a higher likelihood that innovation will succeed when the idea for innovation comes from the union or work group.[51]

Looking at GM's QWL movement, the main objective in the 1970s was that of improved productivity, and improving the quality of work was only a secondary concern when it was started in 1970. With the deterioration in morale, GM's Tarrytown (New York) plant ranked among the worst in terms of both quality and productivity. Responding to this situation, QWL was introduced in two departments to start with in 1971. As introduced, QWL involved both redesigning the workplace and involving workers in process. In 1973, GM signed an agreement with the United Autoworkers (UAW) on introducing QWL. This was the first instance of QWL being specifically included in a labor agreement. In 1977, GM started a program of QWL group training at all of its plants throughout the United States. The results of this program were striking reductions in the incidence of absenteeism and grievances, a smooth transition to production of new models, and a change in Tarrytown from one of the worst GM plants anywhere to one of the best.[52]

Encouraged by this success, GM has changed the objectives of QWL to focus not simply on enhanced productivity but also on enhanced quality of work life, and as of 1981 QWL programs existed in various forms and guises in 95 GM plants.[53] The introduction of QWL has resulted in higher morale and better productivity at both Volvo and GM. However, different results are also possible so long as QWL has the humanization of work as its main objective.

Reviewing the results of ten years of QWL, Richard E. Walton has concluded that work innovation sometimes results in improved productivity and sometimes does not. However, he adds that success is most likely when the two goals of QWL and productivity are pursued equally with no tilt to either side.[54]

QWL in the United States was begun on the assumption that its enactment would be consistent with improved productivity, and it has now been generally accepted by industry. Looking back over the first ten years, Walton says that companies with QWL programs are still in the minority but their numbers are increasing and the movement is now at the bottom of the "S" curve.[55]

Unions, albeit gradually, are shifting from their traditional emphasis on wages, employment, and other factors external to the work itself and becoming increasingly interested in QWL. The agreement between GM and the UAW has already been mentioned, but the UAW also moved in 1973 to include provisions in its contracts with the other leading automobile companies for the establishment of joint labor-management committees.

The labor-management committees were charged with promoting QWL and publicizing the results to other companies.[56] In 1979, representatives of 20 international labor unions met in Washington to discuss labor management cooperation in QWL improvement efforts. Included were representatives from the American AFL-CIO and the U.S. Department of Labor.[57]

In looking at the boom in Japanese studies in the United States, it must be emphasized that this was both a desire to raise productivity and an attempt to find in Japan specific methods for the QWL movement. The interest in Japanese management, which formed the core of the interest in Japan, was an idealistic pursuit of both improved productivity and the humanization of work.

Turning to Japanese Management

The importance of the group is clear from this analysis of American management and the QWL movements. Having discovered the importance of the human factors, American management studies now argue the strategic importance of the group. The group's importance is demonstrated by the informal groups in controlling production in the case of the Hawthorne experiment, the priority of group participation in Likert's theories, and the place of recognition in Maslow's theory. In QWL too, the group is important both in management participation and in self-management. And it was this emphasis on the group that brought many people to look at Japanese management.

The pioneer in this field is James C. Abegglen. As is well known, Abegglen's *The Japanese Factory* focused on the lifetime commitment and the resultant permanent relationship between the firm and the employee as the most critical features distinguishing Japanese and American management.[58]

Peter F. Drucker agrees that the interpersonal relations arising from shared interests and mutual trust are the decisive factor in Japanese management's success.[59]

Yet the work that really brought Japanese management to America's attention was William Ouchi's *Theory Z*. Named in contrast to McGregor's Theory Y, Ouchi's Theory Z is an attempt to take what he sees as the best of Japanese management practices and to apply them to American companies. To begin with, Ouchi divides management into three types (Type J for Japanese management, Type A for American management, and Type Z for something that is not identical to Japanese management but close to it) and argues that each of these types can exist in any country and any culture but that Type J exists in Japan and Types A and Z in the United States and Western Europe.[60] The main features that Type Z should take from Type J are (i) trust among people and groups within the organization and (ii) subtlety with relationships between people, and (iii) intimacy.[61]

However, Type Z differs from Type J in that (i) both assessment and promotions are quick, (ii) both implicit and explicit means of control are used, (iii) the individual bears final responsibility for group decisions, and (iv) the holistic concern (not just for the work but for the total person) is not in a hierarchical relationship but in an egalitarian relationship.[62]

At the risk of over-simplification, the thing that American management wants to learn from Japan is worker involvement in the organization as the core for productivity growth. Backing his claim that Japanese companies are more competitive, Ouchi notes that Japanese firms in the United States have succeeded by adopting Japanese management but American firms in Japan have failed to introduce American management.[63]

Thus it is that the surge of interest in Japanese management stems from the hope that the features that characterize Japanese management (shared interests and mutual trust as expressed in Lodge's communitarianism) can provide solutions for the deterioration in American productivity and hopes that Japanese management can provide practical models for QWL enhancement. It is worth noting in this regard that the Japanese QC circles are widely regarded as the prototype of working group self-management for QWL.

Can Japanese management meet these expectations of it? In the next chapter, I will attempt to outline exactly what Japanese management is and how it has evolved.

Notes

1 *Work in America: Report of a Special Task Force to the Secretary of Health, Education and Welfare,* MIT Press, Cambridge, Mass., 1973, p. 19.

2 *Wall Street Journal,* June 16, 1980.

3 John F. Runcie, "By Days I Make Cars," *Harvard Business Review,* May-June, 1980, p. 107.

4 Daniel Yankelovich, *New Rules: Searching for Self-Fulfillment in a World Turned Upside Down,* Random House, New York, 1981, Chapter 13.

5 *Business Week,* June 4, 1979, p. 152.

6 *Asian Wall Street Journal,* July 17, 1979.

7 *Chicago Tribune,* December 12, 1980.

8 Edwin O. Reischauer, *The Japanese*, Harvard University Press, Cambridge, Mass., 1977.

9 Ezra F. Vogel, *Japan as Number One: Lessons for America*, Harvard University Press, Cambridge, Mass., 1979.

10 George C. Lodge, *The New American Ideology*, Alfred Knopf, New York, 1975, pp. 7-21.

11 Frederick W. Taylor, "The Principles of Scientific Management," in *Scientific Management*, Harper & Row, New York, 1947, pp. 24-25.

12 *Ibid.*, pp. 9-11.

13 Frederick W. Taylor, "Testimony before the Special House Subcommittee," in *ibid.*, pp. 27-30 and p. 192.

14 Frederick W. Taylor, "Shop Management," in *ibid.*, pp. 72-73.

15 Reinhard Bendix, *Work and Authority in Industry*, Harper & Row, New York, 1963, pp. 215-218.

16 Taylor, *op. cit.*, pp. 72-73.

17 Frederick Herzberg, *The Managerial Choice: To Be Efficient and To Be Human*, Dow Jones-Irwin, Homewood, Illinois, 1976, p. 96.

18 F. J. Roethlisberger and William J. Dickson, *Management and the Worker*, Harvard University Press, Cambridge, Mass., 1939, part I.

19 *Ibid.*, part IV.

20 *Ibid.*, Chapter XXVI.

21 Elton Mayo, *The Human Problems of an Industrial Civilization*, MacMillan, 1933, pp. 114-116.

22 Bendix, *op. cit.*, p. 295.

23 Chris Argyris, *Personality and Organization: The Conflict Between System and the Individual,* Harper & Brothers, New York, 1957, Chapter III, especially p. 66.

24 *Ibid.*, pp. 95-97.

25 Rensis Likert, *The Human Organization: Its Management and Value*, McGraw-Hill, New York, 1967, pp. 14-26.

26 *Ibid.*, p. 13 and p. 41.

27 *Ibid.*, pp. 47-52.

28 *Ibid.*, p. 137 and p. 73.

29 A. H. Maslow, *Eupsychian Management*, Richard D. Irwin, Homewood, Illinois, 1965, pp. 1-2.

30 A. H. Maslow, *Motivation and Personality*, Harper & Row, New York, 1954, pp. 35-47.

31 Douglas McGregor, *The Human Side of Enterprise*, McGraw-Hill, New York, 1960, Chapters 3 and 4.

32 *Ibid.*, p. 96.

33 Frederick Herzberg, *Work and the Nature of Man*, Thomas Y. Crowell, New York, 1966, pp. 72-79.

34 *Ibid.*, pp. 144-160.
35 See, for example, Peter F. Drucker, *Management: Tasks, Responsibilities, Practices*, Harper & Row, New York, 1974, pp. 195-196.
36 *Work in America, op. cit.*
37 *Ibid.*, p. 28.
38 Ted Mills, "Europe's Industrial Democracy: An American Response," *Harvard Business Review*, November-December, 1978, pp. 151-252.
39 Richard E. Walton, "How to Counter Alienation in the Plant," *Harvard Business Review*, November-December, 1972.
40 Jerome M. Rosow, "Solving the Human Equation in the Productivity Puzzle," *Management Review*, August 1977.
41 Argyris, *op. cit.*, pp. 177-187.
42 Herzberg, 1976, *op. cit.*, pp. 114-119 and pp. 128-130.
43 Kunio Odaka, *Nihon no Keiei* [Japanese management],Chuo-koron-sha, 1965, p. 171 (in Japanese).
44 Kazuo Koike, *Rodosha no Keieisanka—Seio no Keiken to Nihon* [Management participation for workers—the West European experience and Japan], Nihon Hyoron-sha, 1978, pp. 19-26 and pp. 99-101 (in Japanese).
45 Masumi Tsuda, *Nihonteki Keiei no Yogo* [In defense of Japanese style management], Toyo Keizai Shinpo-sha, 1976, p. 219 (in Japanese).
46 Kunio Odaka, *Sangyoshakaigaku Kogi* [Lectures on industrial sociology], Iwanami Shoten, 1981, p. 222 (in Japanese).
47 Argyris, *op. cit.*, pp. 193-200.
48 Herzberg, 1976, *op. cit.*, pp. 120-122.
49 Pehr G. Gyllenhammar, *People at Work*, Addison-Wesley, Reading, Mass., 1977, p. 54.
50 *Ibid.*, pp. 11-15 and Chapter 3.
51 *Ibid.*, Chapter 4.
52 Robert H. Guest, "Quality of Work Life: Learning from Tarrytown," *Harvard Business Review*, July-August, 1979.
53 *Newsweek*, May 11, 1981, p. 36.
54 Richard E. Walton, "Work Innovations in the United States," *Harvard Business Review*, July-August, 1979, pp. 93-94.
55 *Ibid.*, pp. 93-94.
56 Masaru Ogiwara, *Hatarakigai no Kozo—Nihonteki QWL no Kadai o Saguru* [The will to work — issues of Japanese-style QWL], Daiyamondo-sha, 1979, p. 5 (in Japanese).
57 Paul D. Greenberg and Edward M. Glaser, *Some Issues in Joint Union-Management, Quality of Work Life Improvement Efforts*, W. E. Upjohn Institute for Employment Research, Kalamazoo, Michigan, 1980, p. vii.

58 James C. Abegglen, *The Japanese Factory: Aspects of Its Social Organization*, MIT Press, Cambridge, Mass., 1958.

59 Peter F.Drucker, ''Behind Japan's Success,'' *Harvard Business Review*, January-February, 1981, p. 87.

60 William Ouchi, *Theory Z: How American Business Can Meet the Japanese Challenge*, Addison-Wesley, Mass., 1981, pp. 67-70.

61 *Ibid.*, Chapter 1.

62 *Ibid.*, pp. 71-83.

63 *Ibid.*, pp. 14-15.

Chapter 2

The Changing Face of Japanese Management

Familyism and Welfarism

Japanese management has had three distinct periods. The first period was pre-World War II, when Japanese management was characterized by a family-like atmosphere. The second, which might be called a period of corporate welfarism, was for the first two decades after the war. And the third period, which includes both the rapid growth since the early 1960s and the recessions of the 1970s, was an era of a single-minded emphasis on production.

The most systematic and comprehensive study of the prewar corporate familyism has been done by Hiroshi Hazama, and this section draws heavily upon Hazama's findings.[1]

Basically, this corporate familyism was evolved to adapt the traditional practices of Edo-period (1603-1868) merchants and manufacturers to the changing times. As such, corporate familyism built upon the attitudes ingrained from the labor-management relations that had existed under the samurai-dominated caste society before the Meiji Restoration of 1868. These new labor relationships were consolidated in heavy industry in the second and third decades of this century. This period was also a time when labor relations were changing from the old apprentice system (under which a company would hire leaders who would bring their own helpers) to a system of direct employment for all. As a result, it became important for the company to provide training for the key workers and to take steps to ensure that proprietary technology and other corporate secrets were kept in-house. At the same time, the emerging labor movement forced companies to move to ensure that their workers were "docile ones" with a strong sense of corporate identification. Finally, the sense of international crisis sparked a new emphasis on the traditional ideas of group loyalty, and this also contributed to the spread of corporate familyism.

In this corporate familyism, the functional organization of the company is seen as analogous to the family — and the family is seen as characterized by four main traits: (i) continuity, in that the relations between the family and its constituent members are lifelong or longer, (ii) the priority given to the vertical relationship between parent and child, (iii) combining managing the company as a family business with the linkage between production and consumption, and (iv) giving the family group precedence over the individual.

When this is applied to the corporation, the following five traits emerge: (i) There is a hierarchy (or seniority system) within the corporate social order, usually meaning that there are hierarchal ranking differences between manual and non-manual workers and that there are length-of-service (seniority) distinctions among different classes of employees, with the creation of more specific job distinctions (especially among non-manual jobs) than might be functionally necessary. (ii) Lifetime employment is adopted to bind the employee to the company and to reward loyalty. (iii) Wages are based upon length of service and status, with wages set in accordance with the social hierarchy within the company and supplemental payments to encourage productivity. (iv) Corporate benefits are created to offset wage inadequacies and to give the workers more security, both wages and corporate benefits working together to create what might be called a familistic reward system. (v) There is a strong ideological emphasis on the corporate family, and the belief that the employee's life would be meaningless were it not for the corporation.

It should be noted on the third trait (the fact that wages are determined according to the corporate hierarchy) that there were also special bonuses for hard work, and retirement benefits to encourage production. At the same time, it is worth noting that this system did not apply to temporary or female workers — even though temporary employment served as a very important social safety value after World War I.

This corporate familyism was founded upon a philosophy of paternalism. Within the idea of the corporation as family, the employer was expected to look after his employees and workers were expected to be grateful for this corporate largesse. As such, this was an extension of the paternalism that prevailed prior to the Meiji Restoration of 1868. As Bendix has noted, corporate familyism was an effective answer to "the question of incorporating the newly recruited work force within the economic and political community of the nation which is undergoing industrialization."[2] Under these controls, workers were infused with a strong sense of corporate identification and a strong will to work, despite the wretched working conditions.

Japanese management as it developed after the war is, according to Hazama, different in principle from the prewar corporate familyism and might better be called corporate welfarism. It focuses on employee welfare and is characterized by a theory of harmony between labor and management and even a unity of labor and management. When the postwar ideals rejected prewar practices, employee welfare considerations were emphasized not as familial paternalism but as a management responsibility.[3] Hazama dates the true start of full-blown corporate welfarism in the 1960s.

However, I believe that the humanization of work should be the central tenet of employee welfare. By contrast, productivity was clearly the central goal of harmony and even unity between labor and management as it developed in the 1960s and after. As already explained, enhanced productivity and more humanized work are clearly different goals, and there was only the most superficial concern with QWL during this period of Japanese management, virtually no attention being paid, for example, to job enrichment or other forms of self-actualization. Thus Japanese management in the 1960s and after might better be called productivity-oriented management. More on this later.

As a term, Hazama's "corporate welfarism" is better applicable to the postwar period until 1960. It was during this period that the labor movement, arguably the strongest influence there was on postwar Japanese management, was at its height and at its most insistent in pressing for employee welfare. With management decapitated and disfunctional, it was the labor unions that kept Japanese companies going in the immediate postwar period. As a result, unions were organized and developed not by industry but by company. It was typical of these enterprise unions that they were comprehensive, including both white-collar and blue-collar workers, and in principle all of the company's employees belonged to the union.[4] While management gradually regained its rights and capabilities, the unions concentrated on protecting their members' livelihoods.

In seeking to protect the members' livelihoods, the unions concentrated first on wages and job security.[5] Yet with the decline in corporate activity, wages inevitably fell until they were simply the basic wages needed to ensure a minimum standard of living, and a system of fringe benefits was instituted to offset the low wage levels.[6] And because unemployment would be ruinous to the worker's livelihood, layoffs provoked the fiercest opposition from the unions. This in turn led to the revival of lifetime employment. Here too, temporary workers were tacitly accepted by the unions as outside the system.

With the postwar trend toward democratization, the unions rejected the prewar status hierarchy. The purpose of this was egalitarianism, which was understandable within the context of general impoverishment. Thus it was that Japan abolished the status differences between line and staff people, made wage schedules uniform throughout the company, and developed the practice of standard promotions based upon seniority.[7] In short, the practice of seniority-based rewards was the crystallization of these demands for more uniform treatment of all employees.

It was in this period that the elements said to characterize postwar Japanese management — enterprise unions, lifetime employment, seniority-based rewards, and fringe benefits — were (re)constituted and corporate welfarism was born.

Along with the settling of the postwar confusion and the reestablishment of management rights, the decision-making process also developed in distinctively Japanese ways and took the adjective "groupistic." As the vertical and bureaucratic hierarchy became more entrenched, power was concentrated within a small group of top management people. Because the stockholders had so little real power, there was no way that they or anyone else could check the top management of the company, and it might be noted in this respect that the weakness of the stockholders propelled the company into a mutual-welfare organization. Despite this, the top management very rarely exercised their full power in the decision-making process. Rather, consensus-based collective decision-making became the norm. In this, the group as a whole took responsibility for the decision's ramifications, and top management's responsibility was purely ritualistic.

Because means and ends that would normally be discussed and decided in conference were actually decided through *nemawashi* among a small group of people, the conferences and meetings adopted a consensus style of unanimous decisions. Items which went beyond the meeting's jurisdiction were dealt with through the *ringi* system of policy-making memoranda. This system of having very capable but low-ranking people draw up the plans was used in the early-Meiji government offices and only later adopted in private businesses.[8] Yet decision-making was a very time-consuming process with either meetings or the *ringi* system.

In short, as Frederick Harbison and Charles A. Myers have rightly pointed out, the Japanese company is "a rather unique mixture of highly centralized authoritarianism and democratic-participative management."[9]

The Emerging Emphasis on Higher Productivity

Even though Japanese-style management was common during this period of corporate welfarism, it was largely rejected by the prevailing management ideologies. Rather, there was a strong philosophical current that contended that Japanese-style management was a relic of feudalism and that Japanese companies needed to adopt modern American management methods.

However, the 1965 declaration of the Japanese Committee for Economic Development, the organization of influential managers, came out strongly for reevaluating and positively assessing Japanese management — the first major paper to take this position. Stating that traditional management practices might continue to be effective, this declaration was especially strong in its praise for the intense loyalty to and close identification with the firm that the lifetime employment pattern inspires.[10] This marks a recognition by management that Japanese-style management can play a major role in raising productivity for rapid growth.

The era of rapid growth that began in 1960 created an acute shortage of skilled and young workers, and workers' allegiance to Japanese-style management began to weaken about this same time. Table 2-1 draws upon studies by Odaka to show how company identification has changed over the years at Nippon Kokan. As seen, the percentage of employees identifying with the company fell from half to about one-fourth in the decade 1952-63. At the same time, as shown in Table 2-2, albeit using data from different companies, the support for seniority-based wages also fell from nearly 40 percent in the early 1960s to under 30 percent later in the decade. (I have included the results of the chi-squared test of statistical significance and probability figures when such information is applicable. When the probability is less than 0.05, the data are considered statistically significant, and a probability of less than 0.01 indicates a very high significance.)

Along with the reestablishment of Japanese-style management in the 1960s, there has been a steady trend in labor thinking. As shown in Table 2-3, employee approval of the company at three different companies and three different times showed "very good" at only about 10 percent during both boom times and recessionary times while this was balanced by 10-20 percent negative opinions. These data indicate the impossibility of trying to divide the period since 1960 into sub-periods.

During recessions, the concept of lifetime employment that is supposed to be central to Japanese-style management becomes moot, especially on the production line. While most of the mechanisms for adjusting labor supply and demand are found in the use of temporary help, out-sourcing, and subcontracting, these people and part-time women workers come to account for some of the core labor functions. The fact that these people who are not part of the traditional Japanese-style management concept provide a major part of the labor force marks a clear departure from the philosophy of corporate welfarism.

The pursuit of higher productivity also propelled Japanese corporations along the road to automation and labor-saving, as epitomized by the wholesale introduction of robotics in the 1980s. This attempt to "un-man" most of the production process resulted in driving out large numbers of skilled workers. The result is today's Japanese management — management able to ignore worker interests.

Table 2-1. Company Identification at Nippon Kokan

(unit: %)

	Identify with company	Do not identify with company	Others	Total (Actual)
1952	54.0	18.0	28.0	100.0 (701)
1956	50.0	21.0	29.0	100.0 (1,861)
1960	43.0	28.0	29.0	100.0 (1,051)
1963	26.0	44.0	30.0	100.0 (3,917)

$x^2 = 552.61$ d.f. $= 6$ $p < 0.01$

Source: Kunio Odaka, "Work and Leisure: As Viewed by Japanese Industrial Workers," a paper prepared for the Sixth World Congress of Sociology in Evian, 1966, p.25.

Table 2-2. Percentage of Employees Supporting the Seniority-based Wage System

(unit: %)

Nippon Kokan	Okamura Corp.	Jeco
1960	1966	1967
39	24	28

Source: Based upon data collected by Department of Sociology, University of Tokyo, under the direction of Kunio Odaka.

As productivity enhancement came to be the guiding light of Japanese management, small group activities were introduced on the factory floor. This was the era of the ZD (zero defects) movement, the QC (quality control) circle, the Green Cross (safety) groups, and other groups formed at the shop level with the expectation of full participation by everyone. Particularly conspicuous were QC circles, which sought not only to apply statistical quality control but also to improve the work process and the way work was done.

Classifying these activities into (i) voluntary small group activities for training and education (groups meeting after working hours and regardless of shop assignments), (ii) quasi-self-management shop groups (groups from the same workplace meeting after working hours), and (iii) self-management shop groups (groups from the same workplace meeting during working hours), Odaka has pointed out that it is very difficult to sustain effective voluntary small group activities for training and education, since they tend to get into a rut and are a considerable burden on the member's time, and that the closer a group is to being a self-management shop group the higher the member's morale is likely to be. It was thus only natural that the small group activities tended to gravitate toward officially sponsored in-shop activities.[11]

These small group activities had an astonishing impact on reducing costs, raising productivity, and improving product quality. As a result, most of these small groups were formed, and the movement spread nation-

Table 2-3. Evaluation of Own Company

(unit: %)

	All things considered, is this a good company to work for?						
	A very good company	Quite a good company	About average	Not so good a company	Cannot say it is a good company at all	Uncertain	NA or other
Nippon Kokan (1963)	7	28	42	16	7	*	0
Okamura Corp. (1966)	8	28	41	15	8	*	0
Nissan Motor (1980)	12.8	68.6	*	3.9	3.9	10.3	0.5

Notes: 1. Items marked with asterisks were not asked of those respondents. Same for following tables.

2. It is to be assumed hereinafter that totals are 100% unless otherwise indicated.

3. NA means No answer. Same for following tables.

Source: Data for Nippon Kokan and Okamura Corp. drawn from studies conducted by Department of Sociology, University of Tokyo, under the direction of Kunio Odaka.

wide, at management initiative. It is noteworthy here that these were largely activities held outside of working hours. Under the guise of voluntary activities, they represented an effort to get more work out of employees for the same money. It was thus this realignment of Japanese management and its concentration on improving productivity that enabled Japan to enjoy its rapid economic growth starting in 1960 and to withstand the global recession in the wake of the two oil crises. The secret of this success was therefore seen in the philosophy that even the most inhuman and demeaning work can be demanded of workers so long as wages and other supplemental payments are high enough. And Japanese unions went along with this management emphasis on ever-higher productivity.

Groupism as a Constant

While we have looked at three types of Japanese management (corporate familyism, corporate welfarism, and corporate productivitism), there is broad agreement that the factor underlying all three is groupism. Hazama postulates groupism in contrast to individualism, defining it as "group-oriented (or group-centered) thinking that assigns the group's interests a higher priority than the individual's interests or that makes the value judgement that the group's interests should take precedence over the individual's interests."[12]

It is typical of groupistic values that the emphasis is on harmony. This harmony is a cooperative relationship founded on a long-term balance of the interests of the group's members, and as such it is applicable only when the members themselves are defined.[13]

According to Odaka, groupism may be defined as "a value orientation in which a group or organization ... perceives itself as a close-knit community with a shared destiny and therefore places less emphasis on realizing its members' potential and satisfying their individual aspirations than on ensuring continued well-being of the whole and the overall peace and happiness of the group."[14] Odaka points out that groupistic management practices rest upon the fact that they are consistent with the values and practices of such actual shared-fate groups as the family, village, and feudal clan.[15] In fact, this groupism accounts for the fact that prewar Japanese management was patterned after the family group and that postwar Japanese management was an attempt to build group identification through corporate welfarism. We will look at groupism during the period of productivity-oriented management in the next chapter.

As already noted, the group is strategically important to American management and the QWL movement. In fact, the frantic attention paid to Japanese management was largely because of Japanese management's success with this universal constant of the group. Looking specifically at the relation to QWL, Japanese management's groupistic decision-making was seen as a tool for achieving participative management and organizing small group activities for self-control of work. However, there are a number of distinctively Japanese features to Japanese groupism. Among them, the three main ones are (i) the theory of excessive status consciousness, (ii) excessive identification with the group, and (iii) what might be called exclusionism and group egoism. All three of these factors may thus be seen as impediments to the transplanting of Japanese management practices.

The theory of excessive status consciousness is a theory that, even as it oppresses the individual, demands subservience to the group's vertical hierarchy. Odaka states that this theory of excessive status consciousness arose out of the feudal society's rigid class and occupational stratification and that this was embodied in the precept that everyone should know his station.[16] In actual practice, excessive status consciousness means subservience to rank and the repression of non-ranked talent. Looking first at subservience to rank, all interpersonal contacts are imbued with a strong sense of the individual's relative rank vis-á-vis the other parties. In return for promotions and security, the individual is expected to suppress the self and to serve his superiors. However, in that the hierarchical relationships epitomized by the head of the household and his absolute power are gradually disappearing in Japan, this subservience to rank may not last much longer. Similarly, Japanese groupism is well suited to large numbers of ordinary people, but it has a tendency to repress nonranked talent. While the egalitarianism of wages and other rewards has already been touched upon, it should be noted that there is a strong groupistic spirit that inhibits the truly talented individual from shining on the job as well.

Finally, looking at the excessive identification with the group, Japanese behavior is different from Euro-American behavioral patterns in which the individual takes ultimate responsibility for the results, and responsibility in the Japanese organization is usually defined by the organization or sub-group. This is especially true in the way that the group's goals are defined, and there is a strong belief that they should be defined top-down or should be self-evident from unconditionally held values. And since there is a strong yet intangible climate of oppression pervading the group as a social organ, it is usually impossible for the individual to object to group actions and group goals.

Thus the group identification becomes an all-encompassing web for the total existence of people lacking in self-identification, and the group develops into a shared-destiny group defining the individual's existence. The same is true of the company. The development of the corporation as a shared-destiny group demands excessive group-identification of its members. And because there is little labor mobility, employees are unable to resist these group pressures toward conformity.[17] Moreover, groupism creeps into all aspects of the individual's life. As Eric Hoffer has pointed out in reference to this trend, "under these conditions, it is pertinent to ask whether the collectivism of large-scale enterprises may give rise to a general monstrosity that bosses not only our working hours but invades our homes and dictates our thoughts and dreams."[18]

Third is exclusionism and group egoism. Because Japan's lifetime employment system is premised upon the hiring of new graduates just out of school, it is very difficult for someone to change employers in mid-career. Yotaro Yoshino quotes the young Japanese executives as thinking that "loyalty, to be truly effective, must be based upon feelings and preference."[19] In fact, however, the concept of lifetime employment is more likely sustained only by systemic constraints. According to Hazama, there are large numbers of workers who are kept from changing jobs even though they are very dissatisfied with their work and their employer, and employers are inhibited from firing people by the fear that it could exacerbate labor relations.[20] In fact, lifetime employment is not the norm outside of the giant companies, and lifetime employment has made the Japanese company closed to outside influences.

Corporate egoism is another problem arising along with this exclusionism. Corporate egoism is embodied in the double standard that applies rigid controls and prescribes detailed regulations for behavior within the group yet leaves behavior toward non-group members unregulated and uncontrolled. Corporate groupism is the ideal vehicle for corporate egoism. Corporate behavior based upon excessive competition and ignoring the dictates of social justice is the corporate embodiment of group egoism, and it has its roots in the double standard and ambiguities that pervade not just the company but the whole of society.

Perhaps the prime example of group egoism within the company is the way temporary workers, out-source suppliers, subcontractors, the primarily female part-time work force are treated and used as the employment buffer; and the way that regular full-time employees, with the union in the lead, seek to maintain their preferential status. At the same time and in the same way, factions grow up within the corporation. Chie Nakane has written that the Japanese organization is structured with the leader having vertical lines of contact and control out to a broad range of people throughout the organization, much like the spokes of the traditional Japanese fan.[21] The priority given to these vertical relationships naturally results in factions. Under these conditions, Japanese society characterized by exclusionism and group egoism springs up in clusters throughout the world.

Yet it may be possible to overcome the distinctive parameters of Japanese groupism. If this is possible, it will be confirmed that the parameters of Japanese groupism are not the parameters of groupism *per se*, and the meaning of groupism in its primal form may be discerned.

Notes

1 Hiroshi Hazama, *Nihon Romukanrishi Kenkyu* [Japanese labor management history], Daiyamondo-sha, 1964, Chapter 1 (in Japanese).

2 Reinhard Bendix, *Work and Authority in Industry*, Harper & Row, New York, 1963, p. 441.

3 Hiroshi Hazama, *Nihonteki Keiei* [Japanese style management], Nihon Keizai Shinbun-sha, 1971, pp. 90-98 (in Japanese).

4 Solomon B. Levine, *Industrial Relations in Postwar Japan*, University of Illinois Press, Urbana, Illinois, 1958, Chapter IV.

5 *Ibid.*, pp. 116-120.

6 Shizuo Matsushima, *Romukanri no Nihonteki Tokushitsu to Hensen* [Characteristics of and changes in Japanese labor management], Daiyamondo-sha, 1962, pp. 4-5 (in Japanese).

7 *Ibid.*, p. 343 and Hazama, 1971, *op. cit.*, pp. 87-88.

8 M.Y. Yoshino, *Japan's Managerial System*, MIT Press, Cambridge, Mass., 1968, p. 256.

9 Frederick Harbison and Charles A. Myers, *Management in the Industrial World*, McGraw-Hill, New York, 1959, p. 256.

10 For more details on how this declaration relates to Japanese management see Yoshino, *op. cit.*, pp. 109-111.

11 Kunio Odaka, *Sangyoshakaigaku Kogi* [Lectures on industrial sociology], Iwanami Shoten, 1981, pp. 320-324 (in Japanese).

12 Hazama, 1971, *op. cit.*, p. 16.

13 *Ibid.*, pp. 24-25.

14 Kunio Odaka, *Japanese Management: A Forward-looking Analysis*, Asian Productivity Organization, Tokyo, 1986, p. 29.

15 Odaka, 1981, *op. cit.*, p. 55.

16 Kunio Odaka, *Shokugyokan no Henkaku* [How perception of occupations are changed], Kawaide Shobo, 1944, p. 39 (in Japanese).

17 Peter F. Drucker, "Behind Japan's Success," *Harvard Business Review*, January-February, 1981, p. 236.

18 Eric Hoffer, *The Passionate State of Mind*, Harper & Brothers, New York, 1955, p. 91 (cited by Bendix, *op. cit.*, pp. 239-340).

19 Yoshino, *op. cit.*, p. 235.

20 Hiroshi Hazama, *Igirisu no Shakai to Roshikankei — Hikakushakaigakuteki Kosatsu* [British society and industrial relations — some comparative

sociological observations], Nihon Rodo Kyokai, 1974, p. 194 (in Japanese).

21 Chie Nakane, *Tateshakai no Ningenkankei* [Human relationships in a vertical society], Kodansha, 1966, pp. 114-115 (in Japanese).

Chapter 3

Japanese Companies and Japanese Workers

Low Job Satisfaction

Japanese management is generally viewed as generating a strong sense of job satisfaction, which job satisfaction results in high morale and improved productivity. The truth is that this is just a myth. As will be shown below, Japanese workers are very dissatisfied with their jobs. Despite this, they are highly productive. Normally, one would expect productivity to decline the less satisfaction workers take in their work. However, such is not the case in Japan. Why? Because Japanese management has found ways to resolve this paradox and square the circle.

In this section, comparing the views of Japanese workers at one of Nissan Motor's most advanced plants and American workers at an American Motors plant, I will seek to analyze Japanese workers' attitudes. The comparison is with the United States because that offers the opportunity to highlight the characteristics defining the Japanese situation. For more information about the companies involved and the survey methodology, see the Appendix. It should be noted that when this section refers to "Japanese" and "Americans," it does not mean these entire national populations but means specifically Japanese workers at the Nissan plant and American workers at the American Motors plant.

Let us look first at how satisfied or dissatisfied Japanese workers are with their work. They are not very satisfied. As shown in Table 3-1, most of the American workers are very or fairly satisfied with their work. Nearly 40 percent of the Japanese are very or fairly dissatisfied.

The patterns are the same in Table 3-2's ranking of how satisfied workers are with the use being made of their abilities, Table 3-3's question of whether or not they like their work, and Table 3-4 on whether or not they care about their work. While the majority of the Americans are

Table 3-1. Satisfaction with Job Content

(unit: %)

	How would you rate your satisfaction with the content of your present job?						
	Very satisfied	Fairly satisfied	Moderately satisfied	A little dissatisfied	Very dissatisfied	Uncertain	NA or other
American Motors (United Stated)	23.0	33.6	25.5	12.8	3.6	1.5	0
Nissan Motor (Japan)	4.4	11.8	37.4	28.1	9.9	7.9	0.5

$x^2 = 63.988$ d.f. $= 6$ $p < 0.01$

Table 3-2. Satisfaction with Use of Abilities

(unit: %)

	How would you rate your satisfaction with the use of your abilities in your present job?						
	Very satisfied	Fairly satisfied	Moderately satisfied	A little dissatisfied	Very dissatisfied	Uncertain	NA or other
American Motors (United Stated)	30.2	26.5	22.4	11.2	8.2	1.5	0
Nissan Motor (Japan)	2.0	13.3	34.4	26.1	7.4	16.3	0.5

$x^2 = 60.654$ d.f. $= 6$ $p < 0.01$

very or fairly satisfied with the way their abilities are being used, the bulk of the Japanese are very or a little dissatisfied. Over 80 percent of the Americans, but less than 40 percent of the Japanese, said they like their jobs. And in job-caring, over half of the Japanese said that they used to care more about their jobs while over half of the Americans care just as much about their jobs now as they ever did.

As a result of this low level of job satisfaction, the Japanese workers are much more likely to perceive themselves as simply cogs in a giant machine. According to Table 3-5, nearly two-thirds of Japanese workers but only half of the American workers felt this way. As a result, given the chance to start over, far fewer Japanese would choose the same kind of job they now have. As seen in Table 3-6, only 20 percent of Japanese workers would opt for the same kind of job, while nearly 40 percent of the Americans would.

While all of these factors contribute to the worker's job satisfaction, the total is shown in Table 3-7. In Japan, over two-thirds of the workers are only moderately satisfied or a little dissatisfied with their work. By contrast, over two-thirds of the American workers are very or fairly satisfied. Japanese are clearly less satisfied with their work than Americans are.

Just as Japanese workers are dissatisfied with the motivators they have at work, so are they dissatisfied with wages, working condition, human relations, and the other hygiene factors. Satisfaction with wages is shown in Table 3-8. Fully three-fourths of the American workers are very or fairly satisfied with their wages, but over 80 percent of Japanese workers are only moderately satisfied, a little dissatisfied, or very dissatisfied. The contrast is striking.

Table 3-9 shows satisfaction with job authority and Table 3-10 satisfaction with the opportunities for promotion. The same trends are evident here. Nearly half of the American workers are very or fairly satisfied with their job authority, less than 10 percent of Japanese workers are. Likewise with promotions. Nearly 40 percent of American workers are very or fairly satisfied with the opportunities for promotion, as opposed to less than 6 percent of the Japanese workers. Nor are Japanese workers very satisfied with the interpersonal relations at work. Table 3-11 shows that over 60 percent of American workers are very or fairly satisfied with the human relations at work, but that two-thirds of Japanese workers are fairly or moderately satisfied. The Japanese population is clearly tilted toward the lower end of the satisfaction scale. How superiors treat people is an important part of the interpersonal relations at work. Table 3-12 shows that nearly 60 percent of the American workers agree that their immediate supervisors treat everyone fairly. By contrast, over half of the Japanese workers either say they cannot say one way or the other or say that supervisors are not fair in how they treat people. As seen, compared with American workers, Japanese workers are also very dissatisfied with the outward conditions of their work. How are we to interpret the difference between the American job satisfaction and the Japanese job dissatisfaction?

Argyris says that the apparent high job satisfaction is the result of

Table 3-3. Like or Dislike Work

(unit: %)

	Recently, do you like the work that you have been doing in this company?			
	Like	Uncertain	Dislike	NA or other
American Motors (United States)	84.2	6.6	8.2	1.0
Nissan Motor (Japan)	39.9	45.8	14.3	0

$x^2 = 94.772$ d.f. $= 3$ $p < 0.01$

Table 3-4. Caring About Work

(unit: %)

	I used to care about my work more than I do now.					
	Strongly agree	Agree	Neither agree nor disagree	Disagree	Strongly disagree	NA or other
American Motors (United States)	12.8	21.9	14.8	27.0	23.5	0
Nissan (Japan)	9.9	51.2	31.0	5.9	1.0	1.0

$x^2 = 134.116$ d.f. $= 5$ $p < 0.01$

Table 3-5. Feeling of Being Cog in Machine

(unit: %)

	Have you ever felt as if you were a little gear in a big machine-like organization and felt the meaninglessness of your daily work?			
	Yes	Hardly ever	No	NA or other
American Motors (United States)	50.0	32.7	15.8	1.5
Nissan Motor (Japan)	64.5	15.3	20.2	0

$x^2 = 20.491$ d.f. $= 3$ $p < 0.01$

Table 3-6. Desire to Do Some Other Work

(unit: %)

	If you had a chance to start your career over again, would you prefer the same kind of job as you are doing now?			
	Yes	Uncertain	No	NA or other
American Motors (United States)	37.8	13.3	48.4	0.5
Nissan Motor (Japan)	20.7	28.6	50.7	0

$x^2 = 22.225$ d.f. $= 3$ $p < 0.01$

Table 3-7. Overall Job Satisfaction

(unit: %)

	What is your overall satisfaction with your present job?						
	Very satisfied	Fairly satisfied	Moder-ately satisfied	A little dissatisfied	Very dissatisfied	Uncertain	NA or other
American Motors (United Stated)	25.5	41.3	19.9	9.2	2.6	1.5	0
Nissan Motor (Japan)	2.0	14.8	42.3	26.6	3.0	10.3	1.0

$x^2 = 81.139$ d.f. $= 6$ $p < 0.01$

apathy and disinterest. Not caring, workers are satisfied with their working conditions and are seldom late or absent.[1] Likewise, the *Work in America* report explains that workers who say they are satisfied are actually saying that they are not dissatisfied in Herzbergian terms. Wages and job security are satisfactory, and no expectations of intrinsic reward are betrayed simply because no such expectations exist.[2]

It is true that expectations of work are much higher in Japan than they are in America. Table 3-13 is an attempt to determine why people work, dividing the respondents depending upon whether they see work in terms of its instrumental, bureaucratic, or solidaristic value. While this distinction is one developed by J. H. Goldthope,[3] the questions were devised especially for this survey. According to these results, there is a sharp

Table 3-8. Wage Satisfaction

(unit: %)

	How would you rate your satisfaction with the wages of your present job?						
	Very satisfied	Fairly satisfied	Moder-ately satisfied	A little dissatisfied	Very dissatisfied	Uncertain	NA or other
American Motors (United Stated)	42.4	32.7	16.3	6.1	2.0	0.5	0
Nissan Motor (Japan)	3.0	4.9	36.0	37.8	9.4	8.4	0.5

$x^2 = 165.888$ d.f. = 6 $p < 0.01$

Table 3-9. Satisfaction with Job Authority

(unit: %)

	How would you rate your satisfaction with the authority you can exercise upon your present job?						
	Very satisfied	Fairly satisfied	Moder-ately satisfied	A little dissatisfied	Very dissatisfied	Uncertain	NA or other
American Motors (United Stated)	20.4	26.0	23.5	15.3	9.7	5.1	0
Nissan Motor (Japan)	2.5	7.4	36.9	23.2	5.9	23.6	0.5

$x^2 = 65.476$ d.f. = 6 $p < 0.01$

differentiation between Japan and the United States, most of the American workers seeing work as instrumental. While work is also important instrumentally in Japan, it is almost as important for its solidaristic value, i.e., as a basis for self-identity and social life. The fact that American workers see work more in instrumental terms would tend to substantiate the hypothesis that they are more easily satisfied than Japanese workers are.

However, there are also data indicating that American workers see their jobs as more than mere means. Looking at Table 3-14, somewhat

Table 3-10. Opportunity for Promotion

(unit: %)

	How would you rate your satisfaction with the chances of having a better job in your present company?						
	Very satisfied	Fairly satisfied	Moder-ately satisfied	A little dissatisfied	Very dissatisfied	Uncertain	NA or other
American Motors (United Stated)	16.3	22.5	20.4	16.3	11.2	12.8	0.5
Nissan Motor (Japan)	0.5	5.4	25.1	27.6	10.3	30.1	1.0

$x^2 = 45.811$ d.f. $= 6$ $p < 0.01$

Table 3-11. Satisfaction with Interpersonal Relations at Work

(unit: %)

	How would you rate your satisfaction with the human relations in your present workshop?						
	Very satisfied	Fairly satisfied	Moder-ately satisfied	A little dissatisfied	Very dissatisfied	Uncertain	NA or other
American Motors (United Stated)	23.5	37.8	21.4	10.2	5.6	1.0	0.5
Nissan Motor (Japan)	3.9	25.6	41.9	14.3	6.4	7.4	0.5

$x^2 = 35.388$ d.f. $= 6$ $p < 0.01$

over one-third of Japanese and American workers alike want a job where they can exercise their abilities to the full. Workers in both countries are alike in seeking self-actualization. In this table, the top priority for American workers is job security, but this may be the fluke result of special circumstances in that American Motors was undergoing a period of lay-offs when this survey was conducted.

Regardless of whether it is more Japanese or American workers who

37

Table 3-12. How Fair Supervisors Are

(unit: %)

	My immediate supervisors treat everyone fairly.					
	Strongly agree	Agree	Neither agree nor disagree	Disagree	Strongly disagree	NA or other
American Motors (United States)	18.9	40.8	16.8	18.4	5.1	0
Nissan Motor (Japan)	4.9	39.4	39.9	8.9	5.4	1.5

$x^2 = 41.368$ d.f. $= 5$ p < 0.01

Table 3-13. Reason Why Work

(unit: %)

	I work as an employee of this company, mainly:			
	To get money to support myself and/or my family	To get economic and status career advancement in the organization	To form the basis of my identity and social life	NA or other
American Motors (United States)	84.7	9.7	5.6	0
Nissan Motor (Japan)	51.7	1.5	46.3	0.5

$x^2 = 91.882$ d.f. $= 3$ p < 0.01

see their jobs in instrumental terms, it would seem that the Japanese worker's strong sense of alienation derives from the increasingly inhuman and impersonalized working conditions as Japanese companies pursue productivity enhancement. Runcie's experiences as an autoworker have already been mentioned, but there is also a corollary by Satoshi Kamata reporting on his experiences in a Japanese auto plant.

Kamata, who worked for about half a year as a seasonal worker, reports that there was visible speeding up of the assembly line speed during this period and that all workers had to work at peak levels. There was no creativity or joy in the work, and people were interested only in how much time was left until quitting time. Like Runcie, Kamata thought that

Table 3-14. Definition of Good Job

(unit: %)

	There are many different kinds of jobs in this world. What kind of job do you aspire for? If you were to choose a job at this time, which job would you like to have? (You don't have to consider your present job for this question.)					
	A job where I would receive higher wages	One where employment would be secure and with no fear of lay-off or unemployment	One where I could enjoy spending time with my companions	A job where I could put my full ability into use	Any job where I could serve the public	NA or other
American Motors (United States)	5.1	51.5	3.6	34.7	4.6	0.5
Nissan Motor (Japan)	19.2	15.8	26.6	34.0	3.9	0.5

$x^2 = 113.637$ d.f. $= 5$ $p < 0.01$

Table 3-15. Boredom with Work

(unit: %)

	Do you feel any boredom while you work?					
	Immediately after starting to work	Within an hour after starting to work	Within two hours after starting to work	After two hours of starting to work	Never feel boredom	NA or other
American Motors (United States)	9.7	6.1	9.2	21.9	50.5	2.6
Nissan Motor (Japan)	9.4	2.5	3.4	24.6	59.6	0.5

$x^2 = 30.480$ d.f. $= 5$ $p < 0.01$

this must be punishment for some sin. The result was numerous job-related injuries and a high turn-over rate, and the plant was kept going only with constant infusions of seasonal workers. However, the seasonal workers could quit, while the regular workers were serving life terms.[4]

Productivity and Groupism

In stark contrast to their low level of job satisfaction, Japanese workers are very productive. Table 3-15 asks about on-the-job boredom. Looking at the results, over 70 percent of the American workers said they never get bored or that they only get bored after two hours or longer on the job. For Japanese workers, the figure is even higher — nearly 85 percent. This would seem to indicate that Japanese do not have as much feeling of "putting up with" their work.

By the same token, Table 3-16 uses a question devised by Arthur M. Whitehill and Shin'ichi Takezawa to ask how willingly workers obey the various rules and regulations that the company establishes. As seen, nearly two-thirds of the Japanese workers are willing to obey these rules and regulations and regard violators as undesirable co-workers. On the American side, this is only slightly over 40 percent. It should be noted that these results are in basic agreement with the results found by Whitehill and Takezawa in their research.[5] It is clear that the Japanese worker is more prone to accept the regulations and the way things are structured.

The Japanese workers' attitudes toward productivity as a goal are also clear in their attitudes toward product quality. According to Table 3-17, over 85 percent of Japanese workers say it is never good to have products with defects. The figure for the American workers is less than 70 percent. On the other side of the scale, nearly 20 percent of American workers — as opposed to fewer than 4 percent of Japanese workers — are resigned to turning out defective products from time to time. Likewise, Japanese workers tend to see themselves as primarily responsible for product quality. As seen in Table 3-18, while approximately 70 percent of respondents from both Japan and the United States say that the workers and management are equally responsible for quality, over 20 percent of the Japanese workers say that primary responsibility rests with the workers and over 20 percent of the American workers say it rests with management.

In addition, Japanese workers see their jobs as more of a challenge. In Table 3-19, only about 55 percent of American workers say that their jobs require that they keep learning new things, while the figure for Japanese workers is nearly 70 percent. By contrast, nearly 30 percent of the American workers and less than 10 percent of the Japanese workers say that their jobs do not require them keep learning. As seen, Japanese workers are not quickly bored with their work, are quite willing to obey company rules and regulations, feel responsible for product quality, and think their jobs are challenging. In short, they are in close agreement with Japanese management's ideal of striving for higher productivity.

Yet as seen in the previous section, Japanese workers have a low level of job satisfaction. But the data shown in this section indicate that

Table 3-16. Obedience to Rules and Regulations

(unit: %)

	Regarding rules and disciplinary penalities established by management, I would:				
	Accept such rules and penalities and regard violators as undesirable co-workers	Accept such rules and penalties, but show no ill-feelings against co-workers who violate them	Reluctantly accept such rules and penalties, but speak against them and give moral support to co-workers who violate them	Evade such rules and penalties whenever possible in an attempt to control management's authority over workers' behavior	NA or other
American Motors (United States)	42.4	40.3	6.6	5.1	5.6
Nissan Motor (Japan)	65.1	24.1	5.9	4.4	0.5

$x^2 = 32.908$ d.f. $= 5$ $p < 0.01$

Table 3-17. Attitude toward Product Quality

(unit: %)

	Products you have made either have defects or not. Please check the one that you most agree with.			
	It is never good to have products with defects	It is all right to have some products with defects	It is unavoidable or natural to have products with defects	NA or other
American Motors (United States)	69.3	3.6	17.9	9.2
Nissan Motor (Japan)	85.8	10.8	3.4	0

$x^2 = 48.976$ d.f. $= 3$ $p < 0.01$

Japanese workers are strongly oriented toward productivity. If one accepts that the level of job satisfaction is an indicator of worker morale, it would be logical to conclude that the higher the worker morale the higher the productivity. Yet in the Japanese worker's case, productivity is high even though morale is low.

Table 3-18. Responsibility for Product Quality

(unit: %)

	In your opinion, who is more responsible for the control of quality of your products? Please check the one that you most agree with.			
	Mainly the worker who actually makes products	Both the workers and the management staff	Mainly the management staff	NA or other
American Motors (United States)	6.1	72.0	20.9	1.0
Nissan Motor (Japan)	26.1	68.0	5.9	0

$x^2 = 45.652$ d.f. $= 3$ $p < 0.01$

Table 3-19. Whether Work is Challenging or Not

(unit: %)

	My job requires that I keep on learning new things.					
	Strongly agree	Agree	Neither agree nor disagree	Disagree	Strongly disagree	NA or other
American Motor (United States)	20.9	34.8	16.3	22.4	5.6	0
Nissan Motor (Japan)	12.8	54.6	23.2	6.9	1.5	1.0

$x^2 = 66.442$ d.f. $= 5$ $p < 0.01$

Management theories have demonstrated no consistent correlation between worker attitudes (especially worker job satisfaction) and productivity. However, Argyris has suggested a positive correlation between the two factors, assuming that employees might be trying to maintain their personalities against adverse conditions by opting for minimum satisfaction and minimum production.[6] Likert has also postulated that the discordance between morale and productivity will be mitigated, and that a consistent, positive correlation can be expected if the time factor is taken into consideration.[7] Recognizing that Japanese workers are highly productive despite their poor morale, I see the groupism that is at the heart of Japanese management as resolving this paradox.

Table 3-20 asks workers how well their views are reflected in the company's management. As seen, over 60 percent of American workers feel that their views are not reflected. By contrast, over 80 percent of Japanese workers believe that their views are reflected. This indicates that Japanese management has succeeded in getting the opinions and views of ordinary workers heard at the top.

Likewise, Table 3-21 shows how much say workers feel they have over what changes are made in their workplaces. Over 70 percent of American workers do not think they have much say. By contrast, the largest group in Japan (over 50 percent) is people who cannot say one way or the other, followed by over one-third who feel they have a say. The trends here are very similar to those in Table 3-20 on whether or not the worker's views are reflected in company policy.

All of these results indicate that Japanese management is more successful in finding out what lower-level people think and incorporating these views into company policy. And the data on how much say workers have over their jobs indicate that Japanese management has achieved participative involvement at the shop level.

As a result of this bottom-up style and the sense of participation at the shop level, Japanese workers also evidence a strong trust of management. As shown in Table 3-22, only about 30 percent of American workers say they think they can trust management, while the comparable figure for Japan is over 60 percent. This trust toward management is also behind the worker willingness to obey company rules and regulations.

As the core ideology in Japanese management, groupism shows up clearly as worker identification with the company. As shown in Table 3-23 on what workers think of the company where they work, over 80 percent of Japanese workers think theirs is a good company. Yet this table indicates that American workers also identify strongly with their companies. In the United States too, nearly three-fourths of the workers said theirs was a good company. Even though the company was not doing very well and there was the threat of lay-offs, they evidenced a strong identification with the company.

In seeking to explain this, we might take note of Hazama's observations regarding British workers. Commenting on the strong sense of satisfaction with management and management policies, Hazama notes that (i) people tend to say it is a good company out of self-respect, since they feel they should not continue to work for a company that they are dissatisfied with, (ii) given the fact that the company is limited to a particular segment of the individual's life, the company is evaluated only in terms of how well it functions within that limited realm, (iii) with the high labor mobility, workers respond in terms of what can realistically be expected, and (iv) there is a relatively small disparity between the difficulty of the work

Table 3-20. Influence on Company Policy

(unit: %)

	In this company, are your views well reflected in the company's management?					
	Well reflected	Reflected	Not hardly reflected	Not reflected at all	Uncertain	NA or other
American Motors (United States)	7.7	18.4	29.1	32.6	11.7	0.5
Nissan Motor (Japan)	12.8	68.8	3.9	3.9	10.3	0.5

$x^2 = 173.561$ d.f. = 5 $p < 0.01$

Table 3-21. Influence at Work

(unit: %)

	I have a great deal of say over what changes are made in my work place.					
	Strongly agree	Agree	Neither agree nor disagree	Disagree	Strongly disagree	NA or other
American Motors (United States)	3.1	7.7	16.8	42.8	29.6	0
Nissan Motor (Japan)	3.0	33.5	52.1	8.9	1.5	1.0

$x^2 = 174.956$ d.f. = 5 $p < 0.01$

Table 3-22. Trust of Management

(unit: %)

	Do you think that you can trust the management executives of this company?					
	Can trust very much	Can trust quite well	Uncertain	Can hardly trust	Cannot trust at all	NA or other
American Motors (United States)	4.6	26.5	30.6	25.5	12.8	0
Nissan Motor (Japan)	23.6	36.6	23.6	11.8	3.9	0.5

$x^2 = 73.385$ d.f. = 5 $p < 0.01$

and the worker's own abilities.[8] These same conditions would apply more or less to American workers as well.

In any case, it may be considered demonstrated that Japanese management serves to enhance worker identification with the company. It is this groupism, as demonstrated by the ability to have lower-level views transmitted to the top, the positive assessment of participation at the shop level, the trust of management, and the sense of identification with the company, that is the secret of why Japanese workers are able to achieve high productivity even though they are not very satisfied with their work.

Japanese Management as Seen by Japanese Workers

Given this, what do Japanese workers think of Japanese management? Here too, this can most clearly be described in contrast with American workers. Building upon the results of the previous chapter, this section will look at worker views on enterprise unions, lifetime employment, seniority-based rewards, and fringe benefits.

Looking first at enterprise unions, Table 3-24 compares workers' views of labor relations where they work. As seen, nearly two-thirds of Japanese workers and less than half of American workers think that union and management work well together. On the other side of the spectrum, over 20 percent of American workers and less than 10 percent of Japanese workers feel that the two do not work well together. It seems clear that Japanese workers thinks they have better labor relations. This would seem to indicate that the system of enterprise unions is functioning smoothly.

While there are many possible definitions of lifetime employment, it is operationally defined here as a combination of management assurances that people will not be fired and labor reluctance to job-hop. In surveying worker attitudes, it is thus instructive to ask whether or not they believe management assurances that no one will be fired and labor receptivity to job-hopping.

On the trust of management assurances that no one will be fired, it may be asked how the company handles surplus workers and how satisfied workers are with the assurances of job security. The responses to the question about surplus workers are shown in Table 3-25. Over three-fourths of the American workers said that management will resort to lay-offs in times of trouble. As noted earlier, the company surveyed was actually undergoing a period of lay-offs when the survey was conducted, but the figure still stands in stark contrast to the over 40 percent of Japanese workers who said they were uncertain and the over 30 percent who said the company will not lay people off. Japanese workers clearly put considerable faith in the company's assurances of job security.

Likewise, Japanese workers evidenced a high, and American workers

45

Table 3-23. Opinion of Own Company

(unit: %)

| | Compared with all other companies in general, what do you think of your own company? | | | | | |
	A very good company	Quite a good company	Not so good a company	Cannot say it's a good company at all	Un-certain	NA or other
American Motors (United Sates)	28.6	46.0	10.7	2.0	11.7	1.0
Nissan Motor (Japan)	12.8	68.6	3.9	3.9	10.3	0.5

$x^2 = 46.984$ d.f. = 5 $p < 0.01$

Table 3-24. Views of Labor Relations

(unit: %)

| | In this company the union and management work well together. | | | | | |
	Strongly agree	Agree	Neither agree nor disagree	Disagree	Strongly disagree	NA or other
American Motors (United States)	8.2	40.8	26.0	19.4	4.1	1.5
Nissan Motor (Japan)	16.7	47.8	27.1	4.4	2.5	1.5

$x^2 = 56.043$ d.f. = 5 $p < 0.01$

a low, degree of satisfaction with their present job security. Table 3-26 shows that nearly 60 percent of Japanese workers were very or fairly satisfied with their job security, while this was only slightly over one-fourth for American workers. However, it may be necessary to take these figures at less than face value in view of the fact that there were layoffs in the air when the survey was conducted.

What of the worker willingness to job-hop? As indicated in Table 3-27, the large numbers of American workers willing to switch to a job offering better conditions stands in sharp contrast to the large number of Japanese workers unwilling to change jobs even to get better conditions. In principle, this strong trust of management assurances of job security and the unwillingness to change jobs substantiate the Japanese practice of lifetime employment. However, when asked what they thought about

Table 3-25. Handling of Surplus Workers

(unit: %)

	If your company's business declines, which of the following do you think your company will resort to?			
	The company will reduce the wages of the employees but will not lay them off	Uncertain about what the company will do	The company will lay off some of the employees but will maintain the same wages as before the business slack	NA or other
American Motors (United States)	1.0	21.9	76.1	1.0
Nissan Motor (Japan)	33.0	41.4	24.6	1.0

$x^2 = 123.635$ d.f. $= 3$ $p < 0.01$

Note: Nissan workers were asked not about lay-offs but about firings.

Table 3-26. Satisfaction with Present Job Security

(unit: %)

	How would you rate your satisfaction with the security of your present employment?						
	Very satisfied	Fairly satisfied	Moderately satisfied	A little dissatisfied	Very dissatisfied	Uncertain	NA or other
American Motors (United States)	9.7	17.3	13.8	16.3	24.0	18.9	0
Nissan Motor (Japan)	28.0	30.2	26.0	2.0	0.5	12.8	0.5

$x^2 = 116.625$ d.f. $= 6$ $p < 0.01$

the practice of lifetime employment *per se*, the results, as shown in Table 3-28, are surprisingly similar (although admittedly not the same) for Japanese and American workers. While one would expect the Japanese workers to be much more in agreement with the principle of lifetime employment, the results do not bear this out. In seeking to explain this apparent discrepancy, it may be thought that Japanese workers are becoming increasingly skeptical of lifetime employment the more dissatisfied they are with their

Table 3-27. Willingness to Change Jobs

(unit: %)

	Which of the following views applies to your case?			
	If there were a job with better conditions/terms than my present job, I would readily change my job	Can't say now whether I would change my job or not in case of another better job	Even if there were a job with better terms than my present job, I would not change my job	NA or other
American Motors (United States)	39.3	43.9	14.8	2.0
Nissan Motor (Japan)	26.6	40.9	32.5	0

$x^2 = 22.386$ d.f. $= 3$ $p < 0.01$

Table 3-28. Views on Lifetime Employment

(unit: %)

	In Japan, it can be widely observed that a lifetime employment system is almost a fundamental rule in companies. Below are two opinions about the reasons for the existence of this lifetime employment system: A. The lifetime employment system exists only to allay the fear of unemployment among workers; this way, the workers can assuredly and wholeheartedly pursue their work well. B. Under the lifetime employment system, even if a worker finds a more suitable job or working place elsewhere, he cannot just make the transfer very easily; this way, the workers cannot wholeheartedly pursue their work well. Which of these two views do you agree with?					
	Fully agree with A	Agree with A	Un-certain	Agree with B	Fully agree with B	NA or other
American Motors (United States)	26.0	33.2	24.0	11.2	4.1	1.5
Nissan Motor (Japan)	24.6	38.9	16.3	8.9	10.8	0.5

$x^2 = 67.935$ d.f. $= 5$ $p < 0.01$

own work. Likewise, given the specific conditions prevailing at American Motors at the time of the survey, it may be that American workers were more appreciative than expected of the idea of lifetime employment and guaranteed job security. Whatever the case, it bears noting that one-fifth of the Japanese workers expressed negative feelings about the lifetime employment system. It is thus felt that this weakening of worker identification with the lifetime employment system reflects the changing worker attitudes as Japanese management moves from emphasizing corporate welfarism to emphasizing productivity enhancement.

A question formulated by Ronald Dore[9] to probe opinions on seniority-based rewards yielded the results as shown in Table 3-29. As seen, over 40 percent of Japanese workers agree that a person who has worked for the company longer deserves a higher wage. This is somewhat more than 30 percent who disagreed. By contrast, over 70 percent of American workers disagreed that sensiority should influence wages. When Dore asked the same question in the United Kingdom, he found nearly two-thirds of the British workers disagreed with seniority-based wages.[10] American and British workers are agreed in demanding equal pay for equal work.

Turning back to Japan, the fact that nearly as many people opposed as agreed with the idea that someone with more seniority should be paid better would seem to indicate that there is even more questioning of seniority-based rewards in Japan than there is of lifetime employment. .

Finally, turning to fringe benefits and asking this in relation to wages, it was found, as shown in Table 3-30, that American opinion is polarized with nearly 40 percent of American workers agreeing and over 40 percent disagreeing with the contention that fringe benefits are a desirable form of mutual aid and insurance. By contrast, well over half of the Japanese workers support fringe benefits as desirable even if wages are low.

As seen above, Japanese management as epitomized by enterprise unions,

Table 3-29. Views on Seniority-based Wages

(unit: %)

	Do you think that a person who has served for a long time in the company should receive higher wages than a person with short service, even if they are doing the same work?			
	Yes	Uncertain	No	NA or other
American Motors (United States)	20.9	6.1	72.5	0.5
Nissan Motor (Japan)	43.3	22.2	34.0	0.5

$x^2 = 61.381$ d.f. $= 3$ p < 0.01

Table 3-30. Views on Fringe Benefits

(unit: %)

	Below are two views (A & B) regarding the fringe benefits system that goes with the industry. Which of these two views do you agree with? A. The fringe benefits actually in the final analysis are merely other forms of wages. Therefore, even if the fringe benefits are not sufficient, a higher wage is always more desirable. B. The fringe benefits are forms of mutual aid and insurance. So even if the wage is low and cheap, it is better to have fixed fringe benefits. Please check the statement you agree with:					
	Fully agree with A	Agree with A	Un-certain	Agree with B	Fully agree with B	NA or other
American Motors (United States)	13.3	29.0	20.9	28.1	7.7	1.0
Nissan Motor (Japan)	12.3	13.3	16.7	30.6	26.6	0.5

$x^2 = 62.333$ d.f. $= 5$ $p < 0.01$

lifetime employment, seniority-based rewards, and fringe benefits, is generally supported by Japanese workers. However, doubts are emerging about seniority-based rewards, and even lifetime employment is coming in for questioning.

Still, at the time of the survey, it is clear that the causal structure of Japanese management's leading to groupism in turn leading to high productivity was more than able to make up for the low morale resulting from worker alienation and to sustain Japanese productivity.

Notes

1 Chris Argyris, *Personality and Organization: The Conflict Between System and the Individual*, Harper & Brothers, New York, 1959. pp. 120-121.

2 *Work in America: Report of a Special Task Force to the Secretary of Health, Education and Welfare*, MIT Press, Cambridge, Mass., 1973 pp. 14-17.

3 Hiroshi Hazama, *Igirisu no Shakai to Roshikankei—Hikakushakaigakuteki Kosatsu* [British society and industrial relations—some comparative

sociological observations], Nihon Rodo Kyokai, 1974, pp. 216-217. (in Japanese).

4 Satoshi Kamata, *Japan in the Passing Lane*, Tatsuru Akimoto, trans., Pantheon Books, New York, 1982. Originally published as *Jidosha Zetsubo Kojo,* Kodansha, Gendaishi Kenkyukai, ed., 1973 (in Japanese).

5 Arthur M. Whitehill and Shin'ichi Takezawa, *The Other Worker: A Comparative Study of the Industrial Relations in the United States and Japan*, East-West Center Press, Honolulu, 1972, pp. 113-117.

6 Argyris, *op. cit.*, pp. 120-121.

7 Rensis Likert, *The Human Organization: Its Management and Value*, McGraw-Hill, New York, 1967, Chapter 5.

8 Hazama, 1974, *op. cit.*, pp. 204-208.

9 Ronald Dore, *British Factory—Japanese Factory,* University of California Press, Berkeley, California, 1973, p. 316.

10 *Ibid.*

Chapter 4

Japanese Management in the United States

When Japanese Management Was Not Transplanted

In this chapter, we will look at two Japanese companies (Kikkoman and Sony) that have had manufacturing operations in the United States for at least five years and have succeeded in expanding production and will try to outline their management practices and how workers feel about them, with reference to American Motors as the control American company.

As seen in this and the following section, as of the time of the study, Sony did not try to transplant Japanese management practices to its U.S. operations, but Kikkoman did. As such, the two companies present a good contrast, and study of their practices provides food for thought on whether or not Japanese management transfers and why or why not. However, it should be noted that Sony, even though it eschews Japanese management practices in its U.S. operations, has made a major effort to avoid lay-offs, to promote communication between company and employee, and to create a family-like atmosphere within the company, indicating that it does try to maintain some of the factors said to characterize Japanese management.[1] By way of further explanation, it should be noted that Sony has major production facilities in a West Coast urban location and Kikkoman small production facilities in a Midwestern rural location. For more details on these companies as well as the study methdology, see the Appendix.

In this section, I will concentrate on Sony, a Japanese company that did not transfer Japanese management practices, with special attention to the acceptance or rejection of Japanese management practices, the degree to which groupism was fostered, productivity, and the degree to which the work is made more human.

Looking first at tolerance to Japanese management practices, this was studied in terms of lifetime employment, seniority-based rewards, and fringe

Table 4-1. Willingness to Change Jobs

(unit: %)

	Which of the following views applies to your case?			
	If there were a job with better conditions/terms than my present job, I would readily change jobs	Can't say now whether I would change my job or not in case of another better job	Even if there were a job with better terms than my present job, I would not change jobs	NA or other
Sony (Japanese)	50	41	7	2
Kikkoman (Japanese)	15	62	21	2
American Motors (American)	39.3	43.9	14.8	2.0

Sony-American Motors: $x^2 = 2.576$ d.f. = 3 $0.30 < p < 0.50$
Kikkoman-American Motors: $x^2 = 10.026$ d.f. = 3 $0.01 < p < 0.02$

Table 4-2. Employee Job-hopping

(unit: %)

	If you expect that your company will experience a prolonged decline in business, and if you can get a job with a more prosperous company, would you:				
	Stay with the company and share whatever the future may bring because you have confidence in management	Stay with the company provided that management pledges to try to keep you employed, though perhaps at reduced pay	Stay with the company provided management pledges to try to keep you employed and not reduce your pay	Leave the company and take the job with the more prosperous company	NA or other
Sony (Japanese)	17	7	32	42	2
American Motors (American)	26.5	7.7	51.0	13.3	1.5

$x^2 = 18.901$ d.f. = 4 $p < 0.01$

benefits. Questions about enterprise unions had to be omitted because at the time of the study the company was making a major effort to avoid organization by a national labor union, and this was a very sensitive subject for management and workers alike. Nor were we able to ask about the credibility of management assurances of job security as it relates to lifetime employment. Yet the other side of that coin is the willingness of workers to change jobs. As seen in Table 4-1, there is no statistically significant difference between the workers at Sony and those at American Motors, both companies having a large percentage of workers indicating that they would change jobs. Yet in Table 4-2, over 40 percent of the Sony workers said they were willing to move to a more prosporous company, which is far more than the slightly over 10 percent at American motors. As seen, workers at Sony were more inclined to change jobs than were workers at American motors, which indicates that lifetime employment has not been established at Sony.

The responses on fringe benefits substantiate this finding. As seen in Table 4-3, the largest number of responses was received for health insurance at nearly 50 percent. In second place was unemployment benefits at nearly 30 percent. This indicates that people seek fringe benefits premised upon the assumption that they will change jobs. It should be noted in passing that only 22 percent of American companies have institutionalized systems of employee health insurance.[2] The strong desire for health insurance perhaps reflects the fact that it is so often not available.

Seniority-based rewards are next. As is clear from Table 4-4, there was very strong (over 80 percent) support for seniority-based rewards. This is the exact opposite of the situation generally prevailing in the United States as seen in the previous chapter, and it was probably influenced by the fact that, at the time the survey was conducted, Sony was campaigning to introduce seniority-based rewards in an effort to lower the employee turnover rate. Whatever the causes, seniority-based rewards seems to be one of the easier-to-accept Japanese management practices.

Fringe benefits were asked about in connection with wages, the results shown in Table 4-5. As seen, nearly 70 percent of the Sony respondents preferred high wages to a combination of fringe benefits and lower wages. This is much more than the slightly over 40 percent at American Motors. It is clear that there is little support for Japanese management's emphasis on fringe benefits.

Thus although there was a considerable tolerance for seniority-based wages as part of a pattern of seniority-based rewards, workers rejected lifetime employment and fringe benefits. This is further evidence that Sony did not transplant Japanese management practices.

What of groupism, arguably the core element of Japanese management? What is the situation at Sony? Table 4-6 shows how much employees think their views are reflected in company policy. As seen, over half

Table 4-3. Desired Fringe Benefits

(unit: %)

	Which of the following fringe benefits do you consider most important to you? Please check only one answer.						
	Retire-ment pension	Health in-surance	Work-related accident in-surance	Supple-mentary unem-ploy-ment benefit	Paid holidays and vaca-tions	Savings and stock invest-ment plan	NA or other
Sony (Japanese)	10	46	5	27	7	5	0
Kikkoman (Japanese)	26	43	7	2	11	7	4

$x^2 = 16.608$ d.f. = 6 $0.01 < p < 0.02$

Table 4-4. Views on Seniority-based Wages

(unit: %)

	Do you think that a person who has served for a long time in the company should receive higher wages than a person with short service, even if they are doing the same work?			
	Yes	Uncertain	No	NA or other
Sony (Japanese)	81	7	12	0
Kikkoman (Japanese)	59	11	30	0
American Motors (American)	20.9	6.1	72.5	0.5

Sony-American Motors: $x^2 = 58.667$ d.f. = 3 $p < 0.01$
Kikkoman-American Motors: $x^2 = 30.462$ d.f. = 3 $p < 0.01$

of the Sony people think that management reflects their views, which is far more than the 25 percent or so at American Motors. This indicates that Sony has been rather successful at incorporating bottom-up ideas into management thinking.

As a result, there is strong trust of management. As seen in Table 4-7, over half of the workers at Sony indicate that they trust management. Again this is far more than at American Motors (slightly over 30 percent).

On company identification, Table 4-8 gives the results of asking whether the company is a good company or not. Nearly 80 percent of the workers said that Sony is a good company. However, it should be noted that nearly

Table 4-5. Views on Fringe Benefits

(unit: %)

	Below are two views (A & B) regarding the fringe benefit system that goes with the industry. Which of these two views do you agree with? A. The fringe benefits actually in the final analysis are merely other forms of wages. Therefore, even if the fringe benefits are not sufficient, a higher wage is always more desirable. B. The fringe benefits are forms of mutual aid and insurance. So even if the wage is low and cheap, it is better to have fixed fringe benefits. Please check the statement you agree with:					
	Fully agree with A	Agree with A	Uncertain	Agree with B	Fully agree with B	NA or other
Sony (Japanese)	27	41	7	20	0	5
Kikkoman (Japanese)	15	17	17	38	9	4
American Motors (American)	13.3	29.0	20.9	28.1	7.7	1.0

Sony-American Motors: $x^2 = 20.036$ d.f. = 5 $p < 0.01$
Kikkoman-American Motors: $x^2 = 12.660$ d.f. = 5 $p < 0.01$

three-fourths of the workers at American Motors also said theirs was a good company. While the two figures appear close, the difference lies in the fact that the "very good" responses were nearly 10 percentage points more at Sony than at American Motors, which would seem to indicate a stronger company identification.

As seen, even though Sony has not transplanted Japanese management practices as such, it has still succeeded in fostering a much stronger spirit of groupism than exists at American Motors. In the case of Japanese workers, this groupism made it possible to achieve high productivity despite the low level of job satisfaction. What of Sony?

Product quality is central to productivity. Here, as seen in Table 4-9, nearly half of the respondents thought it was only natural that there should be some defects. This is much more than at American Motors, where the figure was slightly more than 20 percent. The Sony workers do not seem to be very quality-conscious.

Sony attitudes toward productivity may also be seen in their responses on the teaching of new skills and how much opportunity they have to acquire new skills. As seen in Table 4-10, nearly 60 percent of the Sony workers said that they had not learned any new skills in their work. This

Table 4-6. Influence on Company Policy

(unit: %)

	In this company, are your views well reflected in the company's management?						
	Well reflected	Reflect-ed	About average	Hardly reflected	Com-pletely not reflected at all	Un-certain	NA or other
Sony (Japanese)	10	41	20	22	7	*	0
Kikkoman (Japanese)	13	33	17	26	9	*	2
American Motors (American)	7.7	18.4	*	29.1	32.6	11.7	0.5

Sony-American Motors: $x^2 = 22.937$ d.f. = 5 $p < 0.01$
Kikkoman-American Motors: $x^2 = 18.498$ d.f. = 5 $p < 0.01$

Table 4-7. Trust of Management

(unit: %)

	Do you think that you can trust the management executives of this company?						
	Can trust very much	Can trust quite well	About Average	Can hardly trust	Cannot trust at all	Un-certain	NA or other
Sony (Japanese)	20	33	25	15	7	*	0
Kikkoman (Japanese)	17	55	15	4	9	*	0
American Motors (American)	4.6	26.5	*	25.5	12.8	30.6	0

Sony-American Motors: $x^2 = 14.220$ d.f. = 4 $p < 0.01$
Kikkoman-American Motors: $x^2 = 29.126$ d.f. = 4 $p < 0.01$

is in striking contrast to the nearly 70 percent of the workers at Kikkoman who said they had learned new skills.

Table 4-11 gives the results of asking those who had learned new skills what they thought of the way these skills were taught by the company. As seen, less than half of the people who learned new skills at Sony attributed this to the way skills were taught. This is far fewer than at

Table 4-8. Opinion of Own Company

(unit: %)

	Compared with all other companies in general, what do you think of your own company?						
	A very good company	Quite a good company	About	Not so good a company	Cannot say it's a good company at all	Un-certain	NA or other
Sony (Japanese)	37	41	10	0	5	*	7
Kikkoman (Japanese)	63	33	2	2	0	*	0
American Motors (American)	28.6	46.0	*	10.7	2.0	11.7	1.0

Sony-American Motors: $x^2 = 28.982$ d.f. = 5 $p < 0.01$

Kikkoman-American Motors: $x^2 = 16.983$ d.f. = 5 $p < 0.01$

Table 4-9. Views on Product Quality

(unit: %)

	Products you have made either pass during inspection or are rejected. Please check the opinion that you most agree with.			
	It is never good to have rejected products	It is all right to have some rejected products	It is unavoidable or natural to have rejected products	NA or other
Sony (Japanese)	32	17	45	6
Kikkoman (Japanese)	37	9	52	2
American Motors (American)	69.3	3.6	17.9	9.2

Note: Chi-squared test not performed because phrased slightly different for American Motors. See Table 3-17 for actual question.

Kikkoman, where the equivalent figure was three-fourths. Putting together the results of these questions about new skill acquisition, the outlook is pessimistic for further improvements in productivity at Sony.

Having looked at productivity, let us look next at how humanized the work is. There is a very low level of satisfaction with work among workers at Sony. Table 4-12 gives the degree of satisfaction with the

Table 4-10. Skill Acquisition

(unit: %)

	Do you get any new technical skill from your present job?		
	Yes	No	NA or other
Sony (Japanese)	45	44	0
Kikkoman (Japanese)	67	24	9

$x^2 = 11.435$ d.f. = 2 $p < 0.01$

Table 4-11. How New Skills Were Acquired

(unit: %)

	If you got new technical skills from your job, did you get them from being well-taught?	
	Yes	No
Sony (Japanese)	45	55
Kikkoman (Japanese)	75	25

$x^2 = 4.377$ d.f. = 1 $0.02 < p < 0.05$

use being made of the workers' abilities. Here, an astonishing 85 percent of the Sony workers say that the work does not fully utilize their abilities. This is a very high level, compared with the nearly 20 percent at American Motors as seen in Table 3-2. Likewise, the two-thirds who indicated in Table 4-13 that they like the work they are doing is considerably less than the 85 percent who said they liked their work at American Motors.

It is worth noting that, in contrast with the low level of job satisfaction, there is a very strong desire for self-actualization at Sony. Looking at the answers to the kind of work people want to do (Table 4-14), nearly 60 percent of the Sony workers said they wanted work that would let them utilize their abilities to the fullest. This is much higher than the less than 40 percent at American Motors. As seen, the Sony workers have a strong desire for self-actualization yet find that this is not fulfilled and hence have a low level of job satisfaction. It may usually be expected that workers who have a strong desire to use all of their talents and skills would not be satisfied with routine factory work, and the workers at Sony meet these expectations to the hilt. It might also be added that these workers give the lie to the theory of easy-to-please workers mentioned in the previous chapter.

Summing up these findings, although Sony is a Japanese company, it has, with the exception of a certain degree of groupism, generally not sought to transplant Japanese management practices. Productivity at Sony is not generally high, and there is a low level of job satisfaction. The Sony example would thus seem to show that there is little productivity enhancement or job humanization unless Japanese companies take their Japanese management practices with them when they go overseas.

Table 4-12. Utilization of Skills

(unit: %)

	Do you think that your present job fully utilizes your ability?		
	Yes	No	NA or other
Sony (Japanese)	15	85	0
Kikkoman (Japanese)	35	58	7

$x^2 = 8.318$ d.f = 2 $0.01 < p < 0.02$

Table 4-13. Like or Dislike Work

(unit: %)

	Recently, do you like the work that you have been doing in this company?			
	Like	Uncertain	Dislike	NA or other
Sony (Japanese)	63	20	17	0
Kikkoman (Japanese)	87	9	2	2
American Motors (American)	84.2	6.6	8.2	1.0

Sony-American Motors: $x^2 = 11.355$ d.f. = 3 $p < 0.01$
Kikkoman-American Motors: $x^2 = 2.562$ d.f. = 3 $0.30 < p < 0.50$

61

When Japanese Management Was Transplanted

In contrast to Sony, Kikkoman is a Japanese company that succeeded in transplanting its Japanese management practices to its American operations. As in the previous section, we will look at this in terms of the tolerance for Japanese management practices, the degree to which groupism has taken hold, productivity, and the humanization of work. Looking first at the tolerance for Japanese management practices, this includes enterprise unions, lifetime employment, seniority-based rewards, and fringe benefits.

First is the enterprise union. There is no union at Kikkoman, and the company would like to keep the workers from organizing and keep the union out if it can. Thus, as seen in Tables 4-15 and 4-16, nearly 70 percent of the workers do not think that a union is needed, and nearly 60 percent do not think that joining a union would improve their livelihoods. Not only is there no union at Kikkoman, the workers there do not think they need one or would benefit from having one.

Next is lifetime employment. As seen in Table 4-17, workers asked how they thought the company would deal with surplus employees evidenced a strong trust in the company's assurances of job security. Only little more than 20 percent of Kikkoman workers said that the company would lay people off, a figure that is in striking contrast to the more than three-fourths who anticipated lay-offs at American Motors as mentioned earlier, there is much more worker trust of the company at Kikkoman. On whether or not workers would like to change jobs, Table 4-1 shows that only 15 percent of the Kikkoman workers were ready to change jobs if they got a better offer. This is much lower than either the nearly 40 percent at American Motors or the 50 percent at Sony.

This combination of trust in the company's assurances of job security and a reluctance to change jobs indicates that, unlike at Sony, the lifetime employment concept has taken hold at Kikkoman. This conclusion is also substantiated by the kinds of fringe benefits workers want. As shown in Table 4-3, health insurance leads the list at Kikkoman with over 40 percent, but second place is held by retirement pensions at slightly over one-fourth. This indicates that workers want fringe benefits premised on the assumption of lifetime employment. It is also worth noting that only 13 percent of the sample at Kikkoman were 50 years old or older.

As shown in Table 4-4 on seniority-based rewards, nearly 60 percent of the Kikkoman workers favored seniority-based rewards. This is much more than the slightly over 20 percent at American Motors. This indicates that seniority-based rewards are clearly accepted at Kikkoman.

Kikkoman workers were also asked about fringe benefits in connection with wages. The answers are shown in Table 4-5. As seen, nearly half of the Kikkoman workers were willing to opt for good fringe benefits

Table 4-14. Definition of Good Job

(unit: %)

| | There are many different kinds of jobs in this world. What kind of job do you aspire for? If you were to choose a job at this time, which job would you like to have? (You don't have to consider your present job for this question.) | | | | | |
	A job where I would receive higher wages	One where employment would be secure and with no fear of lay-off or unemployment	One where I could enjoy spending time with my companions	A job where I could put my full ability to use	where I could serve the public	NA or other
Sony (Japanese)	17	10	5	59	2	7
Kikkoman (Japanese)	12	39	4	39	4	2
American Motors (American)	5.1	51.5	3.6	34.7	4.6	0.5

Sony-American Motors: $x^2 = 34.411$ d.f. = 5 $p < 0.01$
Kikkoman-American Motors: $x^2 = 5.138$ d.f. = 5 $0.30 < p < 0.50$

Table 4-15. Desire to Join Union (American workers at Kikkoman)

(unit: %)

Which do you think is better for the employees of this company to do, to join a labor union or not to join a labor union?		
Better for this company's employees to join a union	Cannot tell which is better	Better not to join any union at all
11	22	67

Table 4-16. Union's Contribution to Worker Livelihood (American workers at Kikkoman)

(unit: %)

Generally, do you think that labor unions help to improve the life of workers?		
Yes	Uncertain	No
13	30	57

Table 4-17. Handling of Surplus Workers

(unit: %)

	If your company's business declines, which of the following do you think your company will resort to?			
	The company will reduce the wages of the employees but will not lay them off	Uncertain about what the company will do	The company will lay off some of the employees but will maintain the same wages as before the business slack	NA or other
Kikkoman (Japanese)	30	48	22	0
American Motors (American)	1.0	21.9	76.1	1.0

$x^2 = 75.227$ d.f. = 3 $p < 0.01$

Table 4-18. Company Recognition of Job's Importance

(unit: %)

	Does your company recognize the importance of your present work?			
	Yes	Uncertain	No	NA or other
Sony (Japanese)	51	15	34	0
Kikkoman (Japanese)	57	30	11	2
American Motors (American)	50.0	28.1	21.9	0

Sony-American Motors: $x^2 = 4.486$ d.f. = 2 $0.10 < p < 0.20$
Kikkoman-American Motors: $x^2 = 6.945$ d.f. = 3 $0.02 < p < 0.05$

even with low wages. This is much more than the slightly over one-third at American Motors, and it stands in striking contrast to the Sony workers' preference for high wages. As such, it may be said that the Kikkoman workers have accepted the idea of the fringe benefit system. Epitomized by lifetime employment, seniority-based rewards, and fringe benefits, Japanese management practices were generally accepted at Kikkoman, even if they did not have the enterprise union that generally goes with Japanese management. Unlike Sony, Kikkoman has successfully transplanted its Japanese management practices to the United States.

What is the situation at Kikkoman with regard to groupism? Here, it is useful to look at how well workers think that their views are reflected in company policy (Table 4-6), how much they trust management (Table 4-7), and what they think of the company where they work (Table 4-8). Nearly 50 percent of the workers at Kikkoman felt that their views were reflected in company policy. This is much more than at American Motors, but slightly less than at Sony. However, Kikkoman excels in management credibility as over 70 percent of the workers said they trust management, which is far more than at either American Motors or Sony. Finally, on identification with the company, an astounding more than 95 percent of the Kikkoman workers said that Kikkoman is a good company. All of these data tend to indicate that Kikkoman has also succeeded in instilling groupism, and that it has done this even better than Sony.

Given that Kikkoman has succeeded in transplanting Japanese management practices and groupism, what of productivity and job humanization? Productivity can be seen in the attitudes toward product quality (Table 4-9). Like workers at Sony, workers at Kikkoman were not that interested in product quality. These figures would indicate that productivity is not very good at Kikkoman. However, as seen in Table 4-10 and Table 4-11, Kikkoman workers were very positive on the way new skills were taught. This indicates that, even though productivity is currently low at Kikkoman, there is the potential (unlike at Sony) for strong productivity improvements in the future.

What of the work itself at Kikkoman? How much alienation is there, and how satisfied are workers with their work. As seen in Table 4-12, nearly 60 percent of Kikkoman workers felt that they were unable to fully utilize their skills. This is much more than the less than 20 percent of American Motors workers who were dissatisfied with their work as seen in Table 3-2. However, it is still much less than at Sony. Yet when they were asked whether or not they liked their work (Table 4-13), nearly 90 percent of Kikkoman workers said that they liked their work. This is not significantly more than at American Motors and stands in contrast to Sony, which had fewer people liking their work than at American Motors. On whether or not the company recognizes the importance of the worker's work, there was less dissatisfaction at Kikkoman than at either American Motors (over 20 percent) or Sony (over 30 percent). As seen in Table 4-18, only slightly over 10 percent of the Kikkoman workers said that the company does not recognize the importance of their work. In sum, it may be said that there is as much or more job satisfaction at Kikkoman as at American Motors, and Kikkoman is much better in this respect than low-satisfaction Sony. Table 4-14 gives data on the degree to which Kikkoman workers seek self-actualization. As seen, nearly 40 percent want

65

a job that will utilize their full abilities, about the same percentage as want a job with good job security.

As seen, there is somewhat more job satisfaction at Kikkoman than at American Motors – probably because groupism and the other trappings of Japanese management enhance their job satisfaction.

In sum, Kikkoman has generally succeeded in transplanting Japanese management practices to its American operations. As a result, there are signs that productivity is improving, and there is considerable job satisfaction, at Kikkoman. The situation at Kikkoman demonstrates that it is possible for Japanese management to both raise productivity and contribute to humanizing work.

The Significance of Japanese Management in the United States

The Kikkoman example in the previous section would seem to indicate that Japanese management contributes to raising productivity and making the work more human. In this section, we shall look at this question in more detail. However, because the sample sizes are small at both Kikkoman and Sony, these data can only be said to represent trends.

The first issue is that of the humanization of work. There was considerable divergence in replies on the question of whether or not the company recognizes the importance of the work the person is doing. Accordingly, it may be well to focus on this question and compare these answers with the willingness to change jobs. These data are shown in Table 4-19. As seen, there is a very clear positive correlation in both companies between the job satisfaction and the willingness to change jobs. This may be interpreted as meaning that Japanese labor management serves to enhance job satisfaction.

Table 4-19. Correlation between Job Satisfaction and Japanese Management

(unit: actual number)

			Change jobs during recession	
			No	Yes
Company recognition of work's importance	Sony (Japanese)	Yes	15	5
		No	5	9
	Kikkoman (Japanese)	Yes	22	3
		No	10	9

Sony: $x^2 = 5.247$ d.f. $= 1$ $0.02 < p < 0.05$
Kikkoman: $x^2 = 6.808$ d.f. $= 1$ $p < 0.01$

Table 4-20. Comparative Wage Standing

(unit: %)

	How do you compare your present wage with others who do the same job but work in different companies? Please check your answer.					
	My wage is very much higher	My wage is higher	My wage is just about the same as theirs	My wage is lower	My wage is very much lower	NA or other
Sony (Japanese)	2	10	44	29	5	10
Kikkoman (Japanese)	2	9	50	35	2	2

As already seen, Sony had relatively fewer and Kikkoman relatively more workers receptive to Japanese management practices. Thus there was a lower level of job satisfaction at Sony and a higher level of job satisfaction at Kikkoman. Whatever the case, Japanese management, whether seen as practices or as the general adherence to groupism, contributes to enhancing job satisfaction at Kikkoman, and this is one of the major significances of Japanese management in humanizing work. However, there is some doubt about whether or not we can conclude unhesitatingly that Japanese management makes for more humanized work. As seen in the previous chapter, Japanese management in Japan has been a factor enabling the company and workers to improve productivity despite job dissatisfaction with both motivators and hygiene factors. It may well be that the same danger exists in the United States.

It is worth noting the low level of satisfaction with wages, a hygiene factor, at Kikkoman. As seen in Table 4-20, only a little over 10 percent of Kikkoman workers thought that their wages were better than at other companies in the field, and nearly 40 percent thought that they were worse. There was a similar dissatisfaction level at Sony, and both dissatisfaction levels were much higher than the less than 10 percent at American Motors (see Table 3-8). It may thus be concluded that American workers think that Japanese companies pay lower-than-average wages. Even though wages are low and there is considerable dissatisfaction with hygiene factors at Kikkoman, there are signs of improving productivity and there is strong satisfaction with motivating factors at this company that has transplanted Japanese management. In this sense, there is a strong likelihood that Japanese management may tend to productivitism in the United States just as it does in Japan.

Notes

1 Toshio Shishido, Nikko Research Center, ed., *Nihon Kigyo in USA* [Japanese companies in the United States], Toyo Keizai Shinpo-sha, 1980, p. 129 (in Japanese).
2 Linda Rader, *The Application of Japanese Management Techniques in the American South*, (unpublished), 1978, p. 134.

Chapter 5

Japanese Management in Thailand

Rank-and-file Acceptance

This chapter is based mainly on a study done of Thai workers employed at Japanese firms in Thailand, with reference to two other examples of workers under Japanese management: Nissan Motor in Japan and Kikkoman in the United States. It should be noted, however, that this category of Janpanese firms in Thailand is limited to companies with 200 or more employees and includes companies with even minority Japanese equity participation. For details on the methodology, see the Appendix.

There has been a major influx of Japanese companies in Thailand since 1960 as Japanese companies have sought to take advantage of the many incentives and inducements offered for foreign investment. These Japanese firms are an important element in Thailand's industrialization, and they have also provided valuable management experience for Thai citizens. In many cases, given Thailand's relatively agrarian state, the investing Japanese companies have had great difficulty finding, training, and holding the workers that they need, and Japanese companies have often had to provide the bulk of the education their workers need.

As seen in the survey results, over 60 percent of the workers in Japanese manufacturing companies in Thailand are employed in textiles. At the same time and as a result, two-thirds of the workers are women, most of whom are young and do not have much formal education. It was with such workers that Japanese companies have sought to apply Japanese management practices, and their success is indicated by the fact that the worker turnover is relatively low. What impact have Japanese management practices by new Japanese companies had on Thai workers? The survey first looked at the humanization of work as reflected in the data on job satisfaction.

Table 5-1. Importance of Job

(unit: %)

	Do you think that your present job is important for this company?			
	Important	Average importance	Unimportant	NA or other
Thai workers	66.3	31.0	2.7	0
Japanese workers (Nissan Motor)	82.8	10.3	6.9	0

$x^2 = 33.327$ d.f. $= 2$ $p < 0.01$

Note: Thai figures are percentages of the 74.5 percent who gave one of these three answers.

Table 5-2. Company Recognition of Job's Importance

(unit: %)

	Does your company recognize the importance of your present work?			
	Yes	Uncertain	No	NA or other
Thai workers	58.5	33.9	7.6	0
Japanese workers (Nissan Motor)	49.3	30.0	20.2	0.5

$x^2 = 16.959$ d.f. $= 2$ $p < 0.01$

Note: Thai figures are percentages of the 62.9 percent who gave one of these three answers.

Looking first at how important they think their work is for the company, Table 5-1 shows that two-thirds of the Thai workers thought that their work was important for the company. This is much less than the over 80 percent of Japanese workers at Nissan Motor, and it is offset by a contrasting increase in the number of "average importance" replies. Yet when asked whether or not the company is aware of the importance of the work that they do, nearly 60 percent of the Thai workers said the company recognizes their work as important. This is, as shown in Table 5-2, more than the nearly 50 percent of Japanese workers at Nissan Motor. Likewise, far fewer Thai workers said that the company does not appreciate the importance of their work. Likewise, as seen in Table 5-3, nearly 70 percent of the Thai workers expressed satisfaction with their present post, and fewer than 10 percent were dissatisfied. By contrast, as seen in Table 3-7, nearly 30 percent of Japanese workers are dissatisfied with their present post.

Judging from the replies to these three questions, it seems safe to say that Thai workers enjoy a higher level of job satisfaction than Japanese workers do. Like the American workers, most of the Thai workers are satisfied with their work. It is impossible to tell whether or not this is because the Thai workers do not expect much of their jobs, since no data are available on this specific question, but some clues can be gleaned from the data on whether they prefer routine-segmented or total-process work, whether they would prefer higher wages with overtime or lower wages without overtime, and how hard they are pushing for promotion.

Table 5-4 gives the results of asking whether the Thai workers preferred routine-segmented work or total-process work. As seen, 70 percent expressed a preference for total-process work, and only slightly over 20 percent the routine work. On the relationship between wages and overtime, as shown in Table 5-5, nearly 80 percent of the Thai workers said that they preferred a higher wage, even if it meant doing overtime. This is a very high figure. Likewise, as seen in Table 5-6, nearly 90 percent of the workers said that they wanted to work hard and achieve positions of responsibility. It is difficult to conclude from these data that the Thai workers have low expectations toward their work. Rather, it must be concluded that these workers at Japanese companies in Thailand have high aspirations and enjoy a much higher level of job satisfaction than Japanese workers do.

On the question of how productive Thai workers are, data are available on the acquisition of new skills, how well new skills are taught, and whether or not the possibility exists for further training. Looking first at Table 5-7 on the new-skill acquisition, nearly 80 percent of the workers said that they had learned new skills. This is a much higher percentage than for the American workers at Kikkoman. Table 5-8 gives the results of asking if they were able to learn these new skills because they were well taught. As seen, the overwhelming majority said yes, the same as at Kikkoman. Finally Table 5-9 shows that nearly 90 percent of the Thai workers expected to have the opportunity to learn further new skills. This is much more than the over 70 percent at Kikkoman.

These data on skill acquisition also indicate that there is a strong possibility that Thai productivity will improve. Can it then be concluded

Table 5-3. Satisfaction with Present Job (Thai workers)

(unit: %)

Are you satisfied with your present job?		
Yes	So-so	Not really satisfied
69.2	23.3	7.5

Note: Thai figures are percentages of the 81.8 percent who gave one of these three answers.

Table 5-4. Simple vs. Difficult Work (Thai workers)

(unit: %)

The following are Mr. A's and Mr. B's ideas concerning company work: A : Better to do easy work even if it's routine. B : Don't like easy and routine work, and want more of a challenge. What do you think?					
Agree with A	Most likely to agree with A	Most likely to agree with B	Agree with B	Don't know	NA
16.4	6.1	30.7	39.3	6.8	0.7

Table 5-5. Wages and Overtime (Thai workers)

(unit: %)

What is your opinion on the following two ideas concerning the wage and overtime? A : Better to work overtime and get more pay. B : Better to get the regular pay and work the regular time.					
Agree with A	Most likely to agree with A	Most likely to agree with B	Agree with B	Don't know	NA
61.6	16.7	6.1	8.8	5.9	0.9

Table 5-6. Status Aspirations (Thai workers)

(unit: %)

Mr. A and Mr. B have different attitudes toward their way of living.
A : Puts work before personal life and aspires for position of responsibility.
B : Prefers easy work over position of responsibility and takes it easy in everyday living.
Whom do you agree with?

Agree with A	Most likely to agree with A	Most likely to agree with B	Agree with B	Don't know	NA
69.3	18.9	3.7	4.8	2.9	0.4

Table 5-7. Skill Acquisition

(unit: %)

	Do you get any new technical skill from your present office?		
	Yes	No	Don't know/ NA
Thai workers	77.3	7.7	15.0
American workers (Kikkoman)	67	24	9

$x^2 = 13.680$ d.f. = 2 $p < 0.01$

Table 5-8. How New Skills were Acquired

(unit: %)

	If you got new technical skills from your job, did you get them from being well taught?		
	Yes	No	Don't know/NA
Thai workers	57.2	14.0	28.8
American workers (Kikkoman)	50	17	33

$x^2 = 0.931$ d.f. = 2 $p < 0.01$

that, like the case of American workers at Kikkoman, Japanese management serves to give Thai workers a strong sense of job satisfaction and holds the possibility for further productivity improvements? Although the Thai study did not ask any questions touching directly upon Japanese management, such that there are no data addressing this question directly, it did ask whether workers thought seniority-based wages or performance-based wages were preferable and what they thought of the company's welfare benefits. These data are shown in Table 5-10 and Table 5-11. As seen in Table 5-10, nearly half of the Thai workers support seniority-based wages. This is much more than the more than 30 percent that support performance-based wages. It is clear that seniority-based wages have the support of Thai workers.

Turning to Table 5-11, over 30 percent of the Thai workers said that the welfare benefits at the company where they work are good, meaning that they identify strongly with the company. This is 10 percentage points more than the percentage for those who said the welfare benefits were not good. However, it is still a much smaller percentage than at Kikkoman. Still, the data in these two tables would indicate the plausibility of concluding that the Thai workers would support the other facets of Japanese management. In effect, the average worker at Japanese companies in Thailand has accepted Japanese management practices, and this acceptance has helped them to overcome the alienation stemming from their work and to raise their productivity.

Core Worker Rejection

In the previous section, we saw that the average worker at Japanese companies in Thailand is generally satisfied with her work and has the potential for high productivity. However, it is one of the major characteristics of the Thai labor market that there is a strong segment that is unable to adapt to, and hence finds itself critical of, Japanese management practices. In this sense, while the Japanese companies in Thailand have generally succeeded in transplanting Japanese management practices, there is still a definite segment where they have not succeeded. Who are these people, what do they do, and what is their impact on Japanese companies and Japanese management?

Table 5-12 gives the correlations as found with the chi-squared test for the objective factors of sex and educational level and such subjective factors as whether or not the company recognizes the importance of their work, new skill acquisition, and assessment of welfare benefits as they are seen to represent the humanization of work, productivity, and identification with the company. As seen, sex has a 0.005 level of correlation with company recognition, skill acquisition, and assessment of welfare

Table 5-9. Chance for Learning New Skill

(unit: %)

	Do you think you will get any higher technical skill from this company in the future?	
	Yes	No
Thai workers	87.5	12.5
American workers (Kikkoman)	71	29

$x^2 = 6.600$ d.f. = 1 $0.01 < p < 0.02$

Note: Figures are percentages of the 63.2 percent of Thai workers and 76% of American workers at Kikkoman who gave one of these two answers.

Table 5-10. Seniority-vs. Performance-based Rewards (Thai workers)

(unit: %)

Should consider the length of working time only	Should consider the length of working time first and ability and position second	Should consider position and ability first and length of working time second	Should consider only position and ability	Don't know	NA
9.2	37.1	26.3	7.0	6.4	14.0

benefits, and educational background has a 0.005 level of correlation with company recognition and assessment of welfare benefits.

Looking at these findings in more detail, more males than females said that the company does not recognize the importance of their work, indicating that they see the work as less humanized. Table 5-13 gives the breakdown by educational background. As seen, the higher the educational level, the more likely the worker is to say that the company does not recognize the work's importance. This is clear when the responses are compared with the bottom-line figures on the percentage of workers at each educational level.

On the question of whether the worker prefers routine-segmented work or total-process work, there is a 0.05 level of correlation under the chi-squared test between those preferring total-process work and those saying that the company does not recognize the importance of their work. The more the person wants to do total-process work, the more likely he is to say that the company does not recognize the importance of his work.

Putting all of these factors together, the worker likely to have the highest alienation level is a male worker with a strong educational background wanting to do total-process work. These people find it very difficult to be satisfied with the work at Japanese companies.

Looking next at productivity as reflected in the question about new skill acquisition, a higher percentage of males than females said that they acquired new skills. While there was not a 0.05 level of correlation using the chi-squared test, there was a 0.10 level of correlation with educational level, the more education the person had completed the more likely she was to say that she had learned new skills on the job. Thus the better-educated males were more likely to say they had acquired new skills, indicating high productivity.

However, as seen in Table 5-12, better-educated male workers also evidence a strong dissatisfaction with the welfare provisions at Japanese companies, meaning that they have a low level of identification with the company. It may also be thought that this indicates a propensity to reject the Japanese companies. What reasons do these people have for feeling this way?

As noted, alienation is felt most strongly by well-educated male workers. Table 5-14 gives the relations among this feeling of alienation and responses to whether they would prefer seniority-based wages or performance-based wages. As seen, especially in comparison with the bottom-line percentages

Table 5-11. Assessment of Company Welfare System

(unit: %)

	In general, how do you rate the welfare system in this company?			
	Good enough	So-so	Not so good	Don't know/NA
Thai workers	31	31	21	17
American workers (Kikkoman)	68	15	15	2

$x^2 = 26.732$ d.f. = 3 $p < 0.01$

Table 5-12. Chi-squared Test for Job Attitudes (Thai workers)

	Company Recognition	Skill Acquisition	Welfare Assessment
Sex	0.005	0.005	0.005
Education	0.005		0.005

Table 5-13. Job Recognition and Educational Background

(unit: %)

	Never been in school	Primary education	Secondary education	Vocational school	College or university	Total (Actual)
Recognized	0.6	70.8	15.5	10.1	3.0	100.0 (168)
Uncertain	0	59.8	29.9	7.2	3.1	100.0 (97)
Not recognized	0	31.8	31.8	22.8	13.6	100.0 (22)
NA	0.6	73.4	20.1	2.4	3.6	100.0 (169)
Average	0.4	67.6	21.1	7.2	3.7	100.0 (456)

$p < 0.005$

in each group, the less the person feels the company recognized the importance of his work, the more likely he is to feel that performance-based wages are preferable to seniority-based wages. This indicates that male workers with better education are also dissatisfied with Japanese companies and their Japanese management practices as reflected in the seniority-based wage schedules.

In order to probe the reasons for this dissatisfaction among the core workers — meaning the better educated and more experienced workers, the workers the other workers look up to, and the natural leaders in the workplace — a focus group discussion was conducted with six male core workers living in Bangkok. For details on this survey, the methodology, and the subject selection, see the Appendix. All of these people have had

Table 5-14. Job Recognition and Views on Seniroty-vs. Performance-based Rewards (Thai workers)

(unit: %)

	Should consider the length of working time only	Should consider the length of working time first and ability and position second	Should consider position and ability first and length of working time second	Should consider only position and ability	Don't know/ NA	Total (Actual)
Recognized	13.7	50.6	28.0	6.5	1.2	100.0 (168)
Uncertain	9.3	47.4	36.1	2.1	5.1	100.0 (97)
Not recognized	9.1	27.3	40.9	18.2	4.5	100.0 (22)
NA	4.7	18.9	17.2	8.9	50.3	100.0 (169)
Average	9.2	37.1	26.3	7.0	20.4	100.0 (456)

$x^2 = 17.158$ d.f. $= 8$ $0.02 < p < 0.05$ (excluding Don't know/NA)

at least five years of education, they range in age from 25 to 40, and two of them are working or have worked for Japanese firms. This discussion was intended to bring out what Thai core workers thought of Japanese companies.

In order to stimulate active discussion, the moderator started by asking the participants to imagine that they were going to change jobs and if they would want to work for a Japanese, American, or Thai company. Of the six, four said they would prefer an American company and the other two did not express a definite opinion. The two people with Japanese company employment experience were among the four saying they wanted to work for an American company.

The most commonly cited reason was linguistic, including what was termed a communication gap. This will be dealt with in the next chapter. Among the other reasons was that Japanese companies are perceived as paying lower wages than American companies. This is a major reason for not choosing the Japanese company.

Virat (male aged 25-30, married, secondary education, home appliance industry) said, "I would work for the American company because the pay is better. Everybody wants more money to cover his family's expenses. We have to go for the money." This view was supported by most of the others as well, and is supported by the feeling that Japanese companies are in Thailand in search of low-wage workers and profits.

Sompong (male, 25-30, single, college education, chemicals industry) said, "Japanese only invest in Thailand for the low-wage labor."

Prasert (male, 25-30, married, secondary education, Japanese home appliance plant worker) added, "The Japanese are very egotistical in their investment. They just want to wring profits out of us."

Vichai (male, 35-40, married, secondary education, cosmetics) said, "Japanese are selfish and inconsiderate. When they build a plant, they want to put everything in the same place. They may say that it is convenient for workers to be able to work, eat, and sleep all in the same place, but in fact this is a effort to get the workers all together in one place so they can have them work any time."

Virat added, "Japanese are good at advertising and public relations. They say they are going to do this or that, and they get the workers to work hard for them, but in fact they do not do anything. They are great liars."

This may be seen as a reaction to the Japanese company's shift toward productivitism. While these are all elements of the rejection of the Japanese company for hygiene factors, the rejection for motivation reasons is even more important and more serious. In discussing these motivational factors, it is important to note that these core workers feel very superior toward the general workers.

Aroon (male, 30-35, married, vocational education, cosmetics) said, "Uneducated workers do not like the systematic and highly organized factory work. The more we explain it, the less they understand it."

Sompong said, "We have to get the ordinary worker to accept the machines and the machinery system. The ordinary worker is irresponsible, and does not have any sense of how to use money. They do not have any savings because they go out and get drunk after payday."

Vichai said, "The average worker is bound to complain about the rules and regulations that we make, no matter what they are. There are always complaints. But after a while, they accept them. They just do not want to have things forced on them. We have to be tolerant toward the general worker."

Thus a major cause of complaint is that the Japanese staff does not treat them the way they should as skilled employees. Aroon criticizes,

"The Japanese act too important. They should give a little of the credit to the Thai people who work with them. The Japanese are always watching the other employees, but the Thai people do not like to be hassled. Just tell them once, and that's enough." However, it should be noted that there was also a minority view expressed: Sompong said, "In criticizing the Japanese, we have to remember that the Japanese who come to Thailand are in a higher social or professional class than we are. We do not see many non-executive Japanese in Thailand. So it should not surprise us that they feel superior to the Thai workers."

This same point came up in the group discussion with five Thai executives. The discussion was held among executives in Bangkok, three of them in manufacturing and two of them in finance and investment firms. Of the five, two worked for firms that were either joint ventures with Japanese capital or had close relations with Japanese companies. For more information on this group discussion, the participants, and the methodology, see the Appendix.

Boonyasitt (male, 35-40, married, secondary education, investment and finance company, frequent dealings with Japanese companies) said, "The Japanese basically want to be in charge. In any joint venture, when they are passing along technical knowhow, the Japanese see themselves as the aid-givers. The Japanese tend to think that they are doing us a favor or that they know more than we do. In the initial stages of a joint venture, the Japanese do not recognize or acknowledge Thai skills."

Sarinthorn (female, 30-35, single, majored in accounting at university, financial insurance firm) added, "I have a lot of friends who work for joint ventures with Japanese firms. Most of them are frustrated because they do not get promoted even though they are very talented. It is only the Japanese who get promoted to executive positions. There was one well-known Japanese company that promised a friend of mine a lot of money and a position of authority. He is a very talented individual. He gave his all to the company, teaching them everything he knew. About two years later, when they had drained him, the company shifted him to a do-nothing dead-end position. I do not have a single friend or relative who enjoys working with Japanese."

Thus even the Japanese wage system is a cause of dissatisfaction in Thailand, as shown by the following statement that came out of the group discussion among the core workers.

Sompong said, "Americans look at how capable you are and pay you accordingly, but Japanese do not pay much attention to ability."

From these two group discussions, it may be concluded that the tendency among core workers to reject Japanese companies stems not only from the hygiene factor of low wages but also from the motivational factors

Table 5-15. Views on Lifetime Employment

(unit: %)

	In Japan, it can be widely observed that a lifetime employment system is almost a fundamental rule in companies. Below are two opinions about the reasons for the existence of this lifetime employment system: A. The lifetime employment system exists only to allay the fear of unemployment among workers; this way, the workers can assuredly and wholeheartedly pursue their work well. B. Under the lifetime employment system, even if a worker finds a more suitable job or working place elsewhere, he cannot just make the transfer very easily; this way, the workers cannot wholeheartedly pursue their work well. Which of these two views do you agree with? Please check the statement you agree with.					
	Fully agree with A	Agree with A	Un-certain	Agree with B	Fully agree with B	NA
Thai executives	37	33	4	18	8	0
Japanese workers (Nissan Motor)	24.6	38.9	16.3	8.9	10.8	0.5

$x^2 = 23.315$ d.f. = 3 $p < 0.01$

Table 5-16. Views on Seniority-based Wages

(unit: %)

	Do you think that a person who has served for a long time in the company should receive higher wages than a person with short service, even if they are doing the same work?			
	Yes	Uncertain	No	NA
Thai executives	76	2	22	0
Japanese workers (Nissan Motor)	43.3	22.2	34.0	0.5

$x^2 = 20.380$ d.f. = 3 $p < 0.01$

Table 5-17. Attitudes Toward Fringe Benefits (Thai executives)

(unit: %)

"The company welfare system should be improved as much as possible in order to retain the best employees and, in turn, for the company to grow." Do you agree or disagree with this opinion?		
Definitely agree	Can't say for sure	A company's welfare system and a company's growth have no relation at all
84	12	4

Table 5-18. Evaluation of Training in Japan (Thai executives)

(unit: %)

Concerning the training your employees received in Japan, which of the following views do you most agree with?					
Very effective	Somewhat effective	Not very effective	Counter-productive	Undecided	No training in Japan
57	29	6	0	0	8

Table 5-19. Original Work Experience (Thai executives)

(unit: %)

Aside from what you're doing in the joint venture, what would you say is your main line of work? Please choose only one.							
Import-export	Import and domestic sales	Manu-factur-ing	Supply of raw mate-rials	Bank-, ing, insur-ance, or other financial related fields	Work for another foreign capita-lized firm	Govern-ment employee including military and law enforce-ment	Other
2	44	14	0	8	6	8	18

that they feel their talents are not appreciated and their chances for promotion are blocked. This may thus be seen as another manifestation of the fact that the Japanese groupism tends to oppress talented individuals, cited in Chapter 2 as one of the disadvantages of Japanese management. In many cases, this is supported and substantiated by an exclusionist groupism among the Japanese staff, and this will be discussed in the next chapter. Still, the seeming paradox of strong job dissatisfaction and high productivity among Thai core workers was also evident among Japanese workers. In Japan, Japanese management has managed to reconcile these conflicting factors, although the system is fraying at the edges. By contrast, Japanese management does not seem to be working in the case of Thai core workers. Thus these people have the potential for causing major problems for Japanese companies in Thailand.

Joint-venture Partner Acceptance

Based upon the results of surveys with the Thai-side partners in manufacturing joint ventures, this section attempts to discover and delineate their attitudes toward Japanese management. For more information on this survey and the methodology used, see the Appendix.

The survey focused on lifetime employment, seniority-based rewards, and fringe benefits as the three main factors constituting Japanese management and asked the respondents to evaluate each.

As seen in Table 5-15 on the first of these elements, lifetime employment, 70 percent of the respondents supported lifetime employment, most of them strongly. In passing, it should be noted that the same question asked of Japanese workers evoked only about two-thirds support, with far fewer people who said they strongly agreed. The Thai management people indicated more support for lifetime employment than Japanese workers did.

Table 5-16 gives the data on seniority-based wages. As seen, over three-fourths of the people supported the concept of seniority-based wages. Like the previous question, this was also asked of Japanese workers, where it evoked only a little over 40 percent support. Again, just as they did for lifetime employment, the Thai executives show much stronger support for seniority-based wages than the Japanese workers do.

The third element is fringe benefits. As seen in Table 5-17, over 80 percent of the Thai executives supported the idea of improving welfare provisions. When Japanese workers were asked a similar question (Table 3-30), less than 60 percent expressed support for company welfare provisions. Here too, the Thai people are more appreciative of Japanese management than Japanese workers are.

This support for Japanese management also showed up in the discussion with Thai executives.

Suthep (male, 30-35 years old, married, university education, con-

Table 5-20. Company Role (Thai executives)

(unit: %)

	Play a central role	Significant role	Support role	NA
Production	22	24	34	20
Sales	38	22	26	14
Finance	31	29	20	20
Personnel	38	28	20	14
Negotiations with the government, etc.	43	29	20	8

sumer goods) said, "There is much we can learn from Japanese about management control. The Japanese treat their employees very well. Of course, this may be only for the Japanese employees, but it is still good."

Thai executives express strong support for Japanese management, this support substantiated by their views on the training that their employees received in Japan. As seen in Table 5-18, nearly 90 percent of the Thai executives said that they felt the Japanese training provided their employees had been effective.

What accounts for this strong support shown for Japanese management? The first thing that should be pointed out is that most of the Thai joint-venture partners do not have much experience in personnel management at a major production facility. As shown in Table 5-19, nearly half of the joint-venture partners have been importer/exporters or domestic retailers, and less than 20 percent have had experience managing manufacturing facilities.

However, being Thai, they have of necessity had to take a major role in personnel management at the joint ventures. As shown in Table 5-20, the main area in which they play the central role is that of negotiations with the Thai government, with personnel management and sales close behind in a tie for second place. If the figures for "play a central role" and "play a significant role" are combined, negotiations with the government remains in first place and personnel management is clearly in second place. Personnel management is an important area of responsibility for the Thai partners.

In effect, because these Thai partners have to do personnel management even though they have little or no experience in managing a major production facility, they are only too glad to accept and endorse the Japanese management practices established by Japanese corporations.

Chapter 6

Japanese Management in an Alien Cultural Context

How Universal is Excessive Status-consciousness?

So far, we have looked at the impact that the groupism central to Japanese management has on the humanization of work and increasing productivity. In the American and Thai examples, we have seen that transplanting Japanese management generally results in higher productivity and that, in many cases, the work is perceived as more humanized.

In this, it is clear that Japanese management can transplant to other cultures, but since it was conceived and shaped in Japan, Japanese management also includes some elements that are difficult for people in other cultures to accept and that evoke rejection. In section entitled Groupism as a Constant in Chapter 2, these were summarized as (i) excessive status-consciousness, (ii) excessive identification with the group, and (iii) exclusionism and group egoism. In this chapter, we will look at these constraints inherent to Japanese management.

This section looks specifically at excessive status-consciousness. As introduced in Chapter 2, excessive status-consciousness manifests itself as subservience to superiors and lording over subordinates — an emphasis on hierarchy rather than talent. The fact that excessive status-consciousness is not universal was amply shown by the views of the Thai core workers cited in the section entitled Core Worker Rejection in Chapter 5. They indicated considerable frustration at the unwillingness of Japanese companies to recognize their abilities, and they said they were very reluctant to recognize Japanese as their superiors or to obey Japanese.

This rejection of Japanese-style egalitarianism treating everyone the same regardless of ability — which is tantamount to an affirmation of meritocratic policies — is also clearly evident among American workers working at Japanese companies. Some of the discussion below draws upon questions formulated by Whitehill and Takezawa. Using these questions to survey worker attitudes in Japan and the United States, Whitehill and Takezawa found a statistically significant difference between the two. At the same time, workers in Japanese companies in America in our survey differ from both American workers and Japanese workers, demonstrating the influence the Japanese company has on its American employees. The responses to the question by Whitehill and Takezawa concerning what to do about people who are in inappropriate positions (people who have a strong desire to do the job but do not have what it takes) are instructive here. These responses are shown in Table 6-1. While the majority of the Japanese said that the person should be kept on until he retires or dies, over 80 percent of the American workers at Kikkoman opted for continued employment of three months or less. This is much more than the less than 60 percent of average American workers that expressed this view.

Whether they work for Japanese companies or American companies, American workers' expectations of the company's employment policies are clear: not only does dealing harshly with people who cannot do the job not provoke a backlash, failure to act could provoke a backlash. Age-based wages are viewed in much the same way. While it is common in Japan for older people to be higher paid than younger people and age-based wages are the rule, nearly 90 percent of American workers are, as shown in Table 6-2, opposed to this system. There is thus overwhelming opposition to age-based wages, and this is another case in which workers reject the idea of basing wages not on ability but on some non-ability factor such as age. In light of these data, it may be concluded that the theory of excessive status-consciousness as epitomized by obedience to superiors and an unwillingness to be thoroughly meritocratic is not universally accepted by other (non-Japanese) cultures.

Assessment of Group Pressures

In this section, we will look at the second feature of Japanese management that is often difficult for people to accept: the excessive group identification. In order to analyze the pressures that the group brings to bear on the individual in a groupistic environment, it is instructive first to look at the relationship between the private and the public self and then to examine the decision-making process.

Indicative of the relation between one's private and public lives, American workers at Japanese companies in the United States were asked about the relation between their work and their personal lives and about the relation between work and leisure. In addition, Americans working for Japanese firms in the United States and Thai workers working for Japanese firms in Thailand were asked what kind of a boss they would prefer.

Table 6-1. Handling of Unqualified Workers

(unit: %)

	If a worker, although willing, proves to be unqualified on his job, management should feel a responsibility:				
	To continue his employment until he retires or dies	To continue his employment for as long as year so that he may look for another job	To continue his employment for three months so that he may look for another job	To terminate the employment of unqualified workers after about two weeks notice	Other
American workers (Kikkoman)	11	4	42	39	4
Japanese workers	55	23	18	4	0
American workers	23	19	38	20	0

Kikkoman-Japanese: $x^2 = 174.589$ d.f. = 4 $p < 0.01$
Kikkoman-American: $x^2 = 61.264$ d.f. = 4 $p < 0.01$

Note: Data for Japanese and American workers from Arthur M. Whitehill and Shin-ichi Takezawa, *The Other Worker: A Comparative Study of the Industrial Relations in the United States and Japan,* East-West Center Press, Honolulu, 1972, p. 139.

Table 6-2. Opinions on Age-based Wages (at Kikkoman)

(unit: %)

Do you think that a person who is older should receive higher wages than a younger person even if they are doing the same work?		
Yes	Uncertain	No
4	9	87

On Whitehill and Takezawa's question about the relationship between work and personal life, as seen in Table 6-3, almost 60 percent of Japanese workers answered "A part of my life at least equal in importance to my personal life," whereas more than 50 percent of the American workers answered "A place for me to work with management, during work hours, to accomplish mutual goals." Looking at American workers in Japanese companies, almost 40 percent of Sony workers responded with "A part of my life at least equal in importance to my personal life," which is much less from the Japanese response. In contrast, more than 50 percent of the workers at Kikkoman responded with "Strictly a place to work and entirely separate from my personal life." Whether working for Japanese or American companies, Americans generally tend to separate their work from their personal lives, just as Japanese tend to integrate the two.

This same tendency is evident in the responses to Whitehill and Takezawa's question on leisure planning as shown in Table 6-4. At both Sony and Kikkoman, two-thirds of the workers said they favored having the company do the planning for recreational outings but making participation voluntary. This is about the same percentage as Whitehill and Takezawa found with their own survey with Americans. By contrast, this view was supported by only 30 percent of the Japanese. Even when the company makes the plans, the vast majority of American workers at both Japanese and non-Japanese companies favor making participation voluntary. However, about 30 percent of American workers at Japanese companies said "Encourage all workers to participate in company-planned group activities," which was about the same as the figure for Japanese workers.

Whether it is the relationship between work and personal life or the relation between leisure and the company, Americans are quite explicit in separating their public and private selves. This also shows up in Table 6-5 on what kind of boss they prefer. At both Sony and Kikkoman, two-thirds of the workers said they wanted a boss who does not meddle in their private lives or other personal matters but is enthusiastic about providing education and leadership on the job. In Thailand, only about 40 percent of the Thai workers said they wanted a job-oriented boss. On the reverse side of this question, American workers generally did not want a boss who is attentive to their private or personal problems, although the figure was slightly higher at Sony, but nearly 40 percent of the Thai workers wanted such an individual-oriented boss — about the same number as wanted a job-oriented boss. Although the data are old, the results of a 1966 survey at Okamura Corp. are interesting in this connection. At Okamura Corp., the ideal Japanese boss was about mid-way between the Thai and American ideals. At least as seen in these data, it is clear that the American workers strongly prefer a job-oriented boss and are much more vehement than the Japanese in rejecting any meddling in their personal lives. However, it is noteworthy that there is very strong support in Thailand for an individual-oriented boss. Some of the views expressed in the group discussion with core workers are given below.

Table 6-3. Private and Public Lives

(unit: %)

	I think of my company as:				
	The central concern in my life and of greater importance than my personal life	A part of my life at least equal in importance to my personal life	A place for me to work with management, during work hours, accomplish mutual goals	Strictly a place to work and entirely separate from my personal life	Uncertain
American workers (Sony)	0	39	22	27	12
American workers (Kikkoman)	0	4	24	52	20
Japanese workers	9	57	26	8	0
American workers	1	22	54	23	0

Sony-Japanese: $x^2 = 138.932$ d.f. = 4 $p < 0.01$
Sony-Americans: $x^2 = 140.466$ d.f. = 4 $p < 0.01$
Kikkoman-Japanese: $x^2 = 299.251$ d.f. = 4 $p < 0.01$
Kikkoman-Americans: $x^2 = 233.753$ d.f. = 4 $p < 0.01$

Note: Data for Japanese and American workers from Whitehill & Takezawa, *op.cit.*, p. 111.

Vichai said, "I would like my boss to be interested in not just me but my family as well. I think this is important to being a good boss."

Virat added, "I would hope that my boss would understand my family's economic situation and the way we are living, but I do not want him to meddle in private matters."

As seen, the Thai workers draw some very fine distinctions in describing their ideal boss. By educational background, university graduates and primary school graduates want a job-oriented boss, but secondary graduates and vocational school graduates tend to want someone who pays attention to the total person. Likewise, there is a strong correlation between feeling that the company does not recognize the importance of their work and wanting an individual-oriented boss, and between saying that the company does recognize the importance of their work and wanting a job-oriented boss. As seen in the previous section, Thai core workers reject excessive status-consciousness but are willing to accept a certain amount of company interference in their private lives. Reflecting the cultural differences among the United States, Japan, and Thailand, the workers' view of the ideal boss are also non-uniform.

The decision-making process is the second area in which groupistic pressures make themselves felt. As seen in Table 6-6, which uses a question devised by Whitehill and Takezawa to ask about the handling of such personnel problems as promotions, transfers, raises, and working hours,

Table 6-4. Company Recreation

(unit: %)

	With reference to baseball games, picnics, or overnight excursions for workers, it is best for the company to:				
	Require all workers to parti- cipate in company- planned group activites	Encourage all workers to parti- cipate in company- planned group activities	Plan such activities for workers, but leave participa- tion purely voluntary	Let workers plan their own activities	Uncertain
American workers (Sony)	0	34	62	2	2
American workers (Kikkoman)	2	28	68	2	0
Japanese workers	13	32	30	25	0
American workers	1	13	62	24	0

Sony-Japanese: $x^2 = 49.189$ d.f. = 4   p < 0.01
Sony-Americans: $x^2 = 46.555$ d.f. = 4   p < 0.01
Kikkoman-Japanese: $x^2 = 33.126$ d.f. = 3   p < 0.01
Kikkoman-Americans: $x^2 = 17.510$ d.f. = 3   p < 0.01

Note: Data for Japanese and American workers from Whitehill & Takezawa, *op. cit.,* p. 270.

40 percent of the workers at Sony and 50 percent of the workers at Kikkoman expressed support for clearly stated policies in writing. These figures are in basic agreement with the data Whitehill and Takezawa found on American workers in general. By contrast, nearly 50 percent of the Japanese workers opted for discussions whenever a problem arises. This is a clear difference between American and Japanese workers. There are clear differences even between the Japanese companies in the United States, second place going to "the decision of my immediate supervisor" at Sony, where Japanese management has not been introduced, and to group decisions at Kikkoman where Japanese management is the norm. Thus the practice of making decisions in the absence of clear written rules and guidelines is thus not generally accepted in other (non-Japanese cultures), as shown by the fact that it is not supported by American workers.

In this same regard, it is interesting to compare this with the data available on how Thai partners in Japanese joint ventures view the decision-making process. As seen in Table 6-7, there was roughly 50 percent for both consensus decisions in which the issues are discussed well ahead of time through *nemawashi* and everyone has time to work out an agreement they can live with, and majority-rule decision-making in which the issues are hammered out in an open conference. As such, there are strong reservations about the traditional Japanese decision-making pattern of *nemawashi* and consensus-building.

As seen, there are definite problems with trying to make decisions in an unstructured and groupistic way in non-Japanese cultures. There is especially strong reaction among American workers, these people rejecting the over-identification with the group both as it pertains to the relationship between the public and private self and as it is reflected in decision-making. It may be thought that this difference comes out of basic cultural differences between Japan and the United States.

These cultural differences also influence motivational factors (as shown by the responses to questions by Whitehill and Takezawa in Table 6-8). On the question of what motivates them to work, the number-one response given by American workers, whether at Japanese companies or at American companies, was responsibility to company and fellow workers, a very individual-oriented answer. This stands in sharp contrast to the top response among Japanese workers: living up to the expectations of family, friends, and society. However, the number-two responses (promotions at Kikkoman and money at Sony) indicate that Japanese management has been transplanted at Kikkoman but not at Sony.

Groupism is a central tenet of Japanese management, but, as seen in this section, the presence of groupistic pressures is not universally acknowledged or applauded.

Table 6-5. What Kind of Boss is Wanted

(unit: %)

| | Suppose there are two bosses, Mr. A and Mr. B. Mr. A is not a good supervisor but takes very good care of you. Mr. B does not pay attention to workers on personal matters but is active in training and supervising workers to do their work well. With whom would you like to work? | | | |
	Mr. A	Mr. B	Anyone will do	Uncertain or other
American workers (Sony)	27	63	5	5
American workers (Kikkoman)	11	67	15	7
Thai workers	36.4	39.2	12.1	12.3
Okamura Corp. (Japanese)	29	50	19	2

$$\text{Sony + Kikkoman-Thai: } x^2 = 21.626 \quad \text{d.f.} = 3 \quad p < 0.01$$
$$\text{Sony + Kikkoman-Okamura: } x^2 = 20.676 \quad \text{d.f.} = 3 \quad p < 0.01$$
$$\text{Thai-Okamura: } x^2 = 61.888 \quad \text{d.f.} = 3 \quad p < 0.01$$

Notes: 1. Because of the small sample size, Sony and Kikkoman were combined for the chi-squared test.

2. Data for Okamura Corp. collected by Department of Sociology, University of Tokyo, under the direction of Kunio Odaka.

Rejection of Exclusionism and the Communication Problem

While we have looked at the concept of excessive status-consciousness and the excessive propensity to groupism as two issues in Japanese management's non-universality, this section takes up the problem of exclusionism and group egoism.

The fact that Japanese working at Japanese companies in Thailand tend to form exclusive groups and to have little personal interaction with their Thai co-workers, supervisors, or subordinates was a central theme of discussion with the Thai core workers. There were a number of comments on the failure of Japanese staff to fraternize with the local population.

Prasert said, "My Japanese supervisor makes no effort to get to know me personally. The only relations I have with my boss are work-related

Table 6-6. Method of Decision-making

(unit: %)

	Decisions on problems concerning promotion, transfer, wage increases, and hours of work should be made on the basis of:				
	Judgment of the supervisor in charge of the workers involved at the time each such problem arises	Discussions among supervisors and managers concerning each such problem at the time it arises	A general policy which is interpreted in each case by the supervisor in charge of the workers involved	A clearly stated written policy which provides a guide for settling such problems according to pre-determined criteria	Uncertain
American workers (Sony)	22	5	27	41	5
American workers (Kikkoman)	11	28	9	50	2
Japanese workers	5	49	11	35	0
American workers	15	21	4	60	0

Sony-Japanese: $x^2 = 41.821$ d.f. = 4 $p < 0.01$
Kikkoman-Japanese: $x^2 = 30.599$ d.f. = 4 $p < 0.01$
Sony-Americans: $x^2 = 100.331$ d.f. = 4 $p < 0.01$
Kikkoman-Americans: $x^2 = 27.241$ d.f. = 4 $p < 0.01$

Note: Data on Japanese and American workers from Whitehill & Takezawa, *op. cit.,* p. 297.

Table 6-7. Attitudes Toward Decision-making (Thai executives)

(unit: %)

Below are two ways of approaching the managerial policy decision-making process. A. By open debate at a conference, with decisions determined by majority rule. B. By discussing the issues well in advance through *nemawashi,* and arriving at consensus agreement. Which do you agree with?					
Strongly agree with A	Agree with A	Agree with B	Strongly agree with B	Uncertain	NA
28	18	26	24	2	2

relations in the office. I have played golf with many Japanese, but there are some that will not even speak to you later off the golf course."

Virat added, "The only time Japanese take the trouble to talk with us is right after they arrive here. After that, they seem to lose interest. There was one Japanese that I went bowling with and did a lot of other things with right after he got here, but after a couple of weeks he kept telling me he was busy and I hardly saw him at all socially after that."

Warin (male, 25-30 years old, single, technical college graduate, chemicals industry, has worked for Japanese company in the past) said, "Westerners are anxious to get to know us, but Japanese shut us out completely. The Japanese do not seem to have the least interest in associating with us. I worked in a Japanese company for ten years, but I have never been to a Japanese home. I have made an effort to get to know them, even inviting them to my home, but they do not reciprocate."

Seen from the Thai side, the Japanese people in Thailand seem to be a tight-knit group.

Sompong said, "Japanese are only interested in other Japanese, and they do not make an effort to mingle with us."

Aroon complained, "The Japanese do not trust any of us. They get together when we are not there and talk about us behind our backs. I think they are trying to decide if they have let any secrets slip in talking with us."

The exclusionism seems to depend in part on whether the Japanese who are sent to Thailand are engineering people or not.

Table 6-8. Job Motivation

(unit: %)

	I believe workers are willing to work hard on their jobs because:				
	They want to live up to the expectations of their family, friends, and society	They feel it is their responsibility to do whatever work is assigned to them	The harder they work, the more likely they are to be promoted over others to positions of greater responsibility	The harder they work, the more money they expect to earn	Uncertain
American workers (Sony)	7	38	24	29	2
American workers (Kikkoman)	9	43	33	15	0
Japanese workers	41	37	11	11	0
American workers	10	61	9	20	0

Sony-Japanese: $x^2 = 50.927$ d.f. = 4 $p < 0.01$
Kikkoman-Japanese: $x^2 = 30.008$ d.f. = 3 $p < 0.01$
Sony-Americans: $x^2 = 23.756$ d.f. = 4 $p < 0.01$
Kikkoman-Americans: $x^2 = 15.192$ d.f. = 3 $p < 0.01$

Note: Data on Japanese and American workers from Whitehill & Takezawa, *op. cit.*, p. 106.

Virat stated, "There are màny different kinds of Japanese. Japanese supervisors like to talk and fit in very well. But it is hard to get to know the technical and engineering people. The engineers live in a special world all their own."

The exclusionism practiced by Japanese at Japanese firms in Thailand shows up clearly in the personnel management. Japanese personnel assignments are arbitrarily made by the Japanese parent company, and no consideration is given to the needs of the local joint venture.

Virat noted, "Japanese who are assigned to Thailand are transferred after two to four years. Japanese companies send managerial people to Thailand who know nothing about Thailand. And we are very dissatisfied with such managers, because they hold exalted positions even though they know nothing and are largely incapable. Japanese who are sent to Thailand should be specialists. The problems arise when they are not."

The exclusionistic groupism of the Japanese is also reflected in language problems. One of the reasons that core workers said they would rather work for an American firm than a Japanese firm is that it is easier to communicate in English at an American firm.

Aroon said, "I would rather work for an American company. Not only would it pay better, but I think the communication would be easier than it would at a Japanese company because I could use English."

Sompong added, "I think the Japanese companies have good welfare benefits. They are certainly no worse than at the American companies. And even though the pay may be a little less, it is not all that much less. But since all of the technical explanations are in Japanese and not in English, I would rather work for an American company where there was no language barrier."

If Japanese in Thailand have trouble with English, Thai is all the more difficult, and it is the rare Japanese manager who can communicate in Thai.

Virat said, "The Japanese say they will provide technical training, but this is all in Japanese, and we cannot understand a word of it. Japanese should make a greater effort to learn and use Thai."

Vichai said, "Because the Japanese feel superior to us, they think we should speak English with them even though this is Thailand, and they make no effort to use Thai. It may be because their Thai is so bad that they are afraid of being scorned for it."

These are just some of the views that were expressed on the exclusionist tendencies of Japanese managers. These are perhaps summarized in Table 6-9 on how much interaction the ordinary Thai worker at Japanese firms thinks the Japanese have with Thai society. As seen, opinion is divided at somewhat under 20 percent each for "interacts" and "does not interact."

Table 6-9 Japanese Sociability (Thai executives)

(unit: %)

How much do Japanese associate with Thais?				
They like to associate with Thais	So-so	They don't like to associate with Thais	Don't know	NA
18.9	30.9	19.7	16.7	13.8

And there is a significant (0.05 level with the chi-squared test) correlation between those who said the Japanese do not interact with Thai society and those who said that the Japanese cannot be trusted. To sum up, Japanese groupism is manifested in Japanese management practices overseas as the non-universal character traits of exclusionism and group egoism.

Chapter 7

Views of Japan and Japanese Management

Non-correlation between American Views of Japan and Views of Work

In this chapter, we will look at the relationship between how people view Japan and the Japanese and how they view Japanese management. To preview, there does not seems to be any clear correlation between the two among American workers working at Japanese companies, but there is a clear correlation among Thai workers working at Japanese companies. Thus we will look first at the American data and then, in subsequent sections, at the Thai data.

Data were obtained at Kikkoman for how American workers view Japan and the Japanese by asking the respondents to compare the Japanese and American character, to tell which national types they liked, and to estimate the social distance that they feel from Japanese. Table 7-1 gives the results of asking these American workers to compare the Japanese and American characters. As seen, the Japanese score favorably on all traits except that of projecting a somewhat weird, eerie impression. The first-ranking is polite, which was endorsed by two-thirds of the American workers. Second was neat at over 40 percent, and third was kind. By contrast, Japanese were unfavorably rated as eerie by less than one-quarter.

Next, respondents were asked to rank a number of national types in order of their liking for them. These results are shown in Table 7-2. As seen, there was a sharp convergence of views. Ranking from top to bottom, these are British, Japanese, Mexican and Italian, Chinese, Russian, and Nigerian. As seen, Japanese are ranked very favorably.

While these data on personality comparisons and national-type preferences indicated that the American workers think highly of Japanese, the effort was next made to try to determine the strength of these feelings. To do this, we asked a question designed to elicit the social distance from the Japanese with the Bogardus scale as seen in Table 7-3. The data on Japanese views of Americans in this table are taken from a survey conducted by Hiroshi Wagatsuma on how Japanese perceive their own social distance from Americans. As seen, there is strong support for being a good friend or a neighbor, there are increasing reservations about Japanese becoming American citizens or traveling together, and there is strong opposition to intermarriage. Except for the travel aspect, Americans seem to be more accepting than Japanese are, but there is still an arm's length distance.

While the small sample sizes make it impossible to say anything definitive about the order of national-type preferences or the social distance from Japanese, these data are very interesting in indicating that there is very little or no interrelation between these views and the American workers' views of Japanese management, their work, or productivity. In effect, although the American workers still cling to strong national-type stereotypes, these do not influence their opinions of Japanese management. Yet perhaps this is only natural in a country such as the United States, which prides itself on its "cultural pluralism" and where there are large numbers of immigrants from different countries working side by side.

Pro-Japanese and Anti-Japanese among Thai Workers

In Thailand, views of Japan and the Japanese seem to have a considerable correlation with the desire to improve productivity and the degree of job satisfaction. While this will be examined in more detail in the next section, we will look here at the general feelings expressed by Thai workers toward Japan.

First are the views expressed in the group discussion with the core workers.

Vichai said, "The Japanese are always working to schedule. And they are always working. Even after dinner, they are at work away from their families. But we Thai people are more relaxed and leisurely. We do not like everything to be highly structured and organized."

Warin added, "Japanese are very good team players."

Aroon commented, "The Japanese are very self-centered and appear unkind. They are under a lot of psychological stress, and they take that stress out on us because we do not have any escape."

Vichai: "Americans make a genuine effort to understand Thailand, but even if Japanese go to worship at a Thai temple, they are just going through the motions. Because they are so self-centered in their lives, they do not understand other people's feelings."

As seen in these four statements, the first two expressed surprise at the Japanese schedules, hard work, and teamwork, and the other two were

Table 7-1. Comparison of Japanese and American Personality Traits (American workers at Kikkoman)

(unit: %)

Which of the two groups, Americans or Japanese, fit more closely the following descriptions? Please check only one.			
	American	Japanese	NA and uncertain
Kind	22	45	33
Sly and cunning	46	7	47
Polite	4	66	30
Sloven	37	13	50
Neat	9	47	44
Somewhat weird, eerie impression.	20	24	56

eloquent expressions of the impersonalization that results from this hard work and schedule-oriented living.

The data on how much ordinary Thai workers working at Japanese companies trust Japanese are informative here. As seen in Table 7-4, about 16 percent or so said that they felt they could trust Japanese, and nearly 20 percent said that they did not trust Japanese. However, even though there is this widespread distrust of Japanese, it should be noted that Japanese are more trusted than Americans (see Table 7-5).

Compared to these ordinary workers, Thai partners in joint ventures with Japanese companies were much more trustful of Japanese. As seen in Table 7-6, there were virtually no replies saying that they could not trust their Japanese partners. Still, except for people who have Japanese joint venture partners, the average Thai does not seem to trust Japanese that much.

Next we will look at Thai views of Japan as reflected in the views of people working at Japanese companies. To ask their views of Japan, questions were prepared on what foreign countries they liked, how they viewed the future relationship between Japan and the rest of Asia, and what they thought the trends in Thai anti-Japanese feelings would be. Looking first at what country they like, as seen in Table 7-7, Japan ranked top among Thais working at Japanese companies. There were over 20 percent who said they liked Japan, about 10 percentage points more than said they liked the United States. Next in the scoring came West Germany and China.

Table 7-2. Preference for National Types (American workers at Kikkoman)

(unit: %)

Please number the following national types in the order of your feeling of liking for them.

	First	Second	Third	Fourth	Fifth	Sixth	Seventh	Uncertain
British	51	17	0	2	0	0	0	30
Chinese	2	0	0	17	24	11	9	37
Mexican	4	11	22	11	11	4	2	35
Japanese	13	33	17	4	0	0	0	33
Italian	9	4	24	20	7	0	4	32
Russian	2	0	2	2	9	26	22	37
Nigerian	2	0	0	11	11	15	24	37

Table 7-3. Social Distance from Japanese

(unit: %)

What do you think of the following statements?		Agree	Uncertain	Disagree	NA
A Japanese wants you as a good friend.	American workers (Kikkoman)	87	7	4	2
	Japanese	50	43	4	3
$x^2 = 23.646$ d.f. $= 3$ $p < 0.01$					
A Japanese wants to travel with you.	American workers (Kikkoman)	35	35	28	2
	Japanese	37	54	6	3
$x^2 = 24.358$ d.f. $= 3$ $p < 0.01$					
A Japanese wants you as his neighbor.	American workers (Kikkoman)	71	20	7	2
	Japanese	32	57	8	3
$x^2 = 45.680$ d.f. $= 3$ $p < 0.01$					
A Japanese wants to be an American citizen.	American workers (Kikkoman)	37	35	26	2
	Japanese	28	56	13	3
$x^2 = 8.998$ d.f. $= 3$ $0.02 < p < 0.05$					
A Japanese wants to marry your brother, sister, son, or daughter.	American workers (Kikkoman)	24	44	30	2
	Japanese	11	48	36	5
$x^2 = 6.249$ d.f. $= 3$ $0.10 < p < 0.20$ ($p \approx 0.10$)					

Notes: 1. For Japanese, data are social distance from an American.
2. Data on Japan from Hiroshi Wagatsuma and Toshinao Yoneyama, *Henken no Kozo* [The anatomy of prejudice], NHK Publishing, 1967, Chapter 5 (in Japanese).

103

Table 7-4. Trustworthiness of Japanese (Thai workers)

(unit: %)

How much can Japanese be trusted?						
Certainly can be trusted	Can be trusted	So-so	Cannot be trusted	Cannot be trusted at all	Don't know	NA
4.2	12.1	38.8	12.9	6.8	11.4	13.8

Table 7-5. Trustworthiness of Americans (Thai workers)

(unit: %)

How much can Americans be trusted?						
Certainly can be trusted	Can be trusted	So-so	Cannot be trusted	Cannot be trusted at all	Don't know	NA
2.6	4.4	35.5	15.6	5.3	23.0	13.6

Table 7-6. Trustworthiness of Japanese Partners (Thai executives)

(unit: %)

In general, do you think your Japanese partners can be trusted?				
Certainly can be trusted	Can be trusted	So-so	Cannot be trusted	Cannot be trusted at all
54	24	22	0	0

On the future of Japan's relations with the rest of Asia, respondents were asked to choose among the three replies of "Japan will develop in concert with the rest of Asia," "Japan will develop at the rest of Asia's expense," and "Japan will be shut out of Asia." As seen in Table 7-8, slightly under 20 percent forecast co-development and one-quarter said Japan would develop at Asia's expense. Thus there were slightly more expecting Japan to prosper at Asia's expense. These results stand in sharp contrast to the number-one ranking that Japan received in response to the which-country-do-you-like question.

Similarly contradictory results were received to the question of how Thai feelings toward Japan would develop. As shown in Table 7-9, nearly 30 percent of the respondents expected anti-Japanese feelings to intensify, and less than 20 percent expected them to grow weaker. As seen, even though these people expressed a liking for Japan, they believe that Japan will develop at Asia's expense and that anti-Japanese feelings will grow stronger.

What are their views on Japanese companies? Here, there were two questions: one the question of whether or not Japanese companies in Thailand have contributed to raising Thai standards of living and the other on what country they would like to have investment in Thailand. The results of the question on the Japanese companies' contribution to better standards of living are shown in Table 7-10. As seen, over 50 percent said that they have contributed to improving living standards. This is a strongly affirmative response. Likewise, as seen in Table 7-11 on what country they would like to see investing in Thailand, Japan ranks first with nearly one-quarter, followed by the United States with less than 10 percent. This is a strong vote of confidence in Japan. From these results, it seems clear that the Thai people are appreciative of the contribution made by Japanese companies and welcome investment from Japan. However, there were over 20 percent who said they did not want any foreign investment in Thailand.

While these data have provided a look at Thai views of the Japanese, views of Japan, and views of Japanese companies, applying the chi-squared test to determine correlation or non-correlation with the the views of Japan held by Thai workers working at Japanese companies gives the results shown in Table 7-12. As seen, all of the items without exception have a very strong correlation at the 0.05 level or better. And looking at the three questions of whether or not Japanese can be trusted, how Japan's relations with the rest of Asia will develop, and what contribution Japanese companies have made to the Thai standard of living, there is good agreement whether affirmative or negative. Those Thai who harbor distrust of Japanese predict that Japan will develop at Asia's expense and that Japanese companies have not contributed to enhancing Thai living standards.

Given this correlation, it is interesting to try to determine who is favorably inclined toward Japan and who is unfavorably inclined. As seen in the bottom half of Table 7-12, feelings toward Japan seem to be highly correlated with sex, age, and educational background.

Looking first at sex, there is a strong pocket of males saying that Japan will develop at Asia's expense. Likewise, asked about what country they would like to see invest in Thailand, males rejected both Japan and

Table 7-7. Favorite Country (Thai workers)

(unit : %)

Which country do you like best from the list below?

USA	People's Republic of China	West Germany	Japan	Vietnam	Indonesia	USSR	Taiwan	Don't know	NA
12.9	2.9	3.7	22.1	1.3	0.4	0.7	1.1	41.3	13.6

Table 7-8. Future of Japan-Asia Relations (Thai workers)

(unit : %)

What do you think about Japan in Asia in the future?

Japan will cooperate with other Asian countries in development	Japan will progress by exploiting other Asian countries	Other countries will cut off contact with Japan	Don't know	NA
19.3	24.6	2.6	39.5	14.0

Table 7-9. Future of Anti-Japanese Feelings (Thai workers)

(unit : %)

How do you think anti-Japanese feelings in Thailand will develop?

Much stronger	Stronger	Weakened	Much weakened	Don't know	NA
8.8	17.5	13.8	2.4	43.5	14.0

Table 7-10. Perception of Japanese Companies (Thai workers)

(unit: %)

How much do you think Japanese business has contributed in raising the standard of living for Thais in general?

Contribute a lot	Contribute a little	Not sure	Has no contribution	Has no contribution at all	Don't know	NA
11.2	40.8	12.9	2.6	2.9	15.3	14.3

Table 7-11. Welcomed Foreign Investment by Country (Thai workers)

(unit: %)

If there is an increase in foreign investment and foreign corporations, what country would you like this increase to come from?

USA	Japan	Taiwan	Germany	Don't want any at all	Don't know	NA
7.0	23.9	0.2	5.0	23.0	26.9	14.0

Table 7-12. Chi-squared Test for Views of Japan (Thai workers)

	Perception of Japanese company	Japanese trust-worthiness	Japan-Asia relations	Favorite country	Welcome foreign investment	Future of anti-Japanese feeling
Perception of Japanese company						
Japanese trust-worthiness	0.005					
Japan-Asia relations	0.005	0.005				
Favorite country	0.005	0.005	0.005			
Welcome foreign investment	0.005	0.005	0.005	0.005		
Future of anti-Japanese feeling	0.005	0.005	0.005	0.005	0.005	
Sex	0.005	0.005	0.005	0.005	0.005	
Age	0.005	0.005	0.005	0.005	0.005	
Education	0.005	0.005	0.005	0.005	0.005	
Wage		0.005	0.025			0.005

the United States.

By age, there were more young people predicting that Japan would develop at Asia's expense, and middle-aged respondents tended to favor co-development.

The breakdown of views on the future of Japan's relations with the rest of Asia by educational background is given in Table 7-13. As seen, there are slightly more of the less-educated respondents predicting co-development, and far more of the highly educated people forecasting that Japan will prosper at Asia's expense. Likewise, on what country they would like to see invest in Thailand, the less-educated people tend to be pro-Japanese and the more-educated ones pro-American.

Thus it is clear that workers at Japanese companies in Thailand may be divided into pro-Japanese and anti-Japanese groups. The pro-Japanese people are likely to be female, middle-aged, and less well educated, while the anti-Japanese are likely to be male, young, and highly educated. It should be noted that this profile of highly educated young males exactly describes the core workers. Why are the core workers anti-Japanese when the ordinary workers are pro-Japanese? This is the subject of the next section.

The Mechanisms Generating Anti-Japanese Feelings

As seen in Chapter 5, many of the core workers were very negative about how humanized their work is, as reflected in the replies to the question of whether or not the company recognizes the importance of their work. They were also negative on the company's welfare provisions, thought to be an indicator of company identification. Yet they were at the same time, affirmative on the issue of new skill acquisition as an indicator of productivity.

How do these views relate to the views of Japan and the Japanese as seen in the preceding section? These relations are shown in Table 7-14. As seen, responses to the question of whether or not the company recognizes the importance of their work has a strong 0.005 correlation with the chi-squared test for all questions relating to their feelings about Japan. This is the strongest correlation seen. It is thus instructive to focus on this question and its relation to views of Japanese, views of Japan, and views of Japanese companies. In the analysis that follows, those who answered that the company recognizes their work, that it does not, or that they cannot say one way or the other are each treated as 100 percent.

Looking first at their views of Japanese, the correlation between opinions on whether or not the company recognizes the importance of their work and whether or not Japanese can be trusted is shown in Table 7-15. As seen, half of the people who feel unappreciated expressed a distrust of Japanese, and virtually none said they trusted Japanese. By contrast,

Table 7-13. Educational Background and Views of
Japan-Asia Relations (Thai workers)

(unit: %)

	Japan will progress by exploiting other Asian countries	Japan will cooperate with other Asian countries in development	Other countries will cut off contact with Japan	Don't know/ NA	Total (Actual)
Vocational school or more	64.0	20.0	2.0	14.0	100.0 (50)
Junior high school	51.8	17.6	1.2	29.4	100.0 (85)
Elementary school or less	13.8	24.2	3.8	58.2	100.0 (260)
Average	28.4	22.3	3.0	46.3	100.0 (395)

$P < 0.005$

few of the people who felt the company appreciated their work expressed a distrust of Japanese. This suggests that the fact that the person feels the company does not appreciate the importance of his work leads him to develop a distrust of Japanese. The same trend is evident in views of Japan, as the people who feel unrecognized tend not to like Japan. The relationship between feeling that their work is appreciated and their answers to the second question relating to their views of Japan, that of how relations between Japan and the rest of Asia will develop, is shown in Table 7-16. As seen, most of the people who feel unrecognized believe that Japan will develop at Asia's expense, while a plurality of those who feel recognized forecast co-development. Here too, it would seem possible that the lack of recognition at work has led to a general distrust of Japan. This same trend is also evident in the responses to what they think will happen in Thai feelings toward Japan. The people who do not feel recognized think that anti-Japanese sentiment will grow stronger.

Let us look next at the relationship between whether or not they feel the company recognizes the importance of their work and how they view the Japanese company. The relation between on-job recognition and whether or not they think Japanese companies have contributed to improving Thai standards of living is shown in Table 7-17. As seen, fully

Table 7-14. Chi-squared Test for Views of Japan and Job Attitudes

	Perception of Japanese company	Japanese trustworthiness	Welcome foreign investment	Favorite country	Future of anti-Japanese feeling	Japan-Asia relations
Job importance	0.005	0.005	0.005	0.01	0.025	0.01
Job recognition	0.005	0.005	0.005	0.005	0.005	0.005
Job satisfaction	0.005	0.005	0.005	0.025		0.005
Seniority pay	0.005	0.005			0.005	0.005
Simple vs. difficult work	0.005	0.005				0.025
Acquiring new skills		0.05			0.005	0.05
Welfare system assessment	0.005	0.005	0.005	0.005		0.005

Table 7-15. Job Recognition and Japanese Trustworthiness (Thai workers)

(unit: %)

	Certainly can be trusted and can be trusted	So-so	Cannot be trusted and cannot be trusted at all	Don't know/ NA	Total (Actual)
Recognized	36.3	38.7	14.3	10.7	100.0 (168)
Uncertain	8.2	48.5	32.0	11.3	100.0 (97)
Not recognized	0	45.5	50.0	4.5	100.0 (22)
NA/Other	3.0	32.5	14.2	50.3	100.0 (169)
Average	16.3	38.8	19.7	25.2	100.0 (456)

$p < 0.005$

Table 7-16. Job Recognition and Japan-Asia Relations (Thai workers)

(unit: %)

	Japan will cooperate with other Asian countries in development	Japan will progress by exploiting other Asian countries	Other countries will cut off contact with Japan	Don't know/ NA	Total (Actual)
Recognized	32.1	26.8	3.6	37.5	100.0 (168)
Uncertain	23.7	29.9	4.1	42.3	100.0 (97)
Not recognized	4.5	54.5	0	41.0	100.0 (22)
NA/Other	5.9	15.4	1.2	77.5	100.0 (169)
Average	19.3	24.6	2.6	53.5	100.0 (456)

$p < 0.005$

one-third of the people who do not feel appreciated say that Japanese companies have not contributed to improving Thai living standards — a view shared by less than 10 percent of the other categories of respondents.

Table 7-17. Job Recognition and Perception of Japanese Companies (Thai workers)

(unit: %)

	Contribute a lot and contribute a little	Not sure	Little contribution and no contribution at all	Don't know/ NA	Total (Actual)
Recognized	75.6	8.3	4.2	11.9	100.0 (168)
Uncertain	61.9	21.6	6.2	10.3	100.0 (97)
Not recognized	41.0	13.6	31.8	13.6	100.0 (22)
NA/Other	24.3	12.4	3.0	60.3	100.0 (169)
Average	52.0	12.9	5.5	29.6	100.0 (456)

$p < 0.005$

By contrast, three-fourths of those workers who feel appreciated at work said that Japanese companies contributed to raising Thai living standards. Here too, the same process seems to be at work as was evident in their views of Japan and the Japanese.

As seen in Table 7-18 on what country they would welcome investment from, only slightly over 10 percent of the people who do not feel the company appreciates how important their work is said they welcomed investment from Japan. This is much less than the average of over 20 percent or the figures of over 40 percent for people who felt appreciated in their work. This too would seem to indicate that the feeling of being unrecognized at work fosters a bias against Japanese investment.

As seen, the less the person feels the company appreciates his work, the more likely he is to be anti-Japanese. The job dissatisfaction at Japanese companies translates into a dislike of Japan overall.

The anti-Japanese feelings of the core workers also result in a sharp deterioration of their company identification. In the survey of Thai workers, company identification was seen in terms of their assessment of the employee welfare benefits. Thus it is instructive here to look at relations between evaluations of welfare benefits and feelings toward Japanese reflected in their feelings toward the Japanese, Japan, and the Japanese company. As with the question on whether or not the company recognized the importance of the worker's job, the analysis here deals only with those who said good, bad, or average to the question of employee welfare benefits.

Table 7-18. Job Recognition and Welcome Foreign Investment (Thai workers)

(unit: %)

	USA	Japan	Taiwan	West Germany	Don't want any at all	Don't know/ NA	Total (Actual)
Recognized	8.9	43.5	0	3.0	21.4	23.2	100.0 (168)
Uncertain	7.2	16.5	0	10.3	35.0	31.0	100.0 (97)
Not recognized	4.5	13.6	0	13.6	45.6	22.7	100.0 (22)
NA/Other	5.3	10.1	0.6	3.0	14.8	66.2	100.0 (169)
Average	7.0	23.9	0.2	5.0	23.0	40.9	100.0 (456)

$p < 0.005$

Looking first at their views of the Japanese, the relationship between trust of Japanese and assessment of welfare benefits is shown in Table 7-19. As seen, over 40 percent of those who said that the welfare benefits were not good, meaning those who have a low level of identification with the company, expressed a distrust of Japanese, and not even 10 percent said they trusted Japanese. By contrast, nearly 40 percent of the people who identified strongly with the company said they trusted Japanese. It seems reasonable to assume that the deterioration in company identification contributes to heightening distrust of Japanese.

On views of Japan *per se,* Table 7-20 shows the relationship between company identification and foreign country preferences. As seen, only slightly over 15 percent of those with a low level of company identification said they liked Japan. While this is much less than the over 40 percent for people with high levels of company identification, it is also well below the average of over 20 percent. Here too, it would seem that people with a weak company identification tend to develop a dislike of Japan.

Next is their views of Japanese companies as expressed by their assessment of the Japanese companies' contribution to raising Thai standards of living. Of the people with low levels of company identification, 12.5 percent said that Japanese companies did not contribute to raising Thai

Table 7-19. Welfare Benefit Assessment and Japanese Trustworthiness (Thai workers)

(unit: %)

	Certainly can be trusted and can be trusted	So-so	Cannot be trusted and cannot be trusted at all	Don't know/ NA	Total (Actual)
Good enough	37.9	37.1	9.3	15.7	100.0 (140)
So-so	7.9	53.3	23.7	15.1	100.0 (139)
Not so good	9.4	42.6	41.7	6.3	100.0 (96)
Don't know and other	1.2	12.3	4.9	81.6	100.0 (81)
Average	16.3	38.8	19.7	25.2	100.0 (456)

$p < 0.005$

living standards. This is much more than either the 4.3 percent for people identifying strongly with the company or the average of 5.5 percent (Table 7-21). Like their views of Japanese and Japan, their views of the Japanese company seems to be negatively influenced by their low level of company identification.

As seen in Table 7-14, the level of satisfaction with welfare benefits showed a very strong 0.005 level of correlation on the chi-squared test with all questions dealing with feelings toward Japan except that of the future of Thai anti-Japanese feelings. The same trends are thus evident in the other questions that were not discussed in detail here. People who take a dim view of Japan, the Japanese, and Japanese companies also have a low level of satisfaction with welfare benefits. It is clear that anti-Japanese feelings are related to the lack of identification with the Japanese company.

However, the trends are somewhat different when feelings toward Japan and productivity are compared. As seen in Table 7-14, feelings toward Japan do not correlate nearly as well with new skill acquisition as they do with job-recognition and welfare benefit assessment. This would seem to indicate that new skill acquisition takes place irrespective of feelings

Table 7-20. Welfare Benefit Assessment and Favorite Country (Thai workers)

(unit: %)

	USA	People's Republic of China	West Germany	Japan	Vietnam	Indonesia	USSR	Taiwan	Don't know/ NA	Total (Actual)
Good enough	15.7	3.6	1.4	42.2	0.7	0	0	0.7	35.7	100.0 (140)
So-so	16.5	5.0	4.3	18.0	1.4	1.4	0.7	1.4	51.1	100.0 (139)
Not so good	13.5	1.0	9.4	15.6	2.1	0	2.1	2.1	54.3	100.0 (96)
Don't know and other	1.2	0	0	2.5	1.2	0	0	0	95.1	100.0 (81)
Average	12.9	2.9	3.7	22.1	1.3	0.4	0.7	1.1	54.9	100.0 (456)

$p < 0.005$

Table 7-21. Welfare Benefit Assessment and Perception of Japanese Companies (Thai Workers)

(unit: %)

	Contribute a lot and contribute a little	Not sure	Little contribution and no contribution at all	Don't know/ NA	Total (Actual)
Good enough	67.1	10.0	4.3	18.6	100.0(140)
So-so	54.7	18.7	5.0	21.6	100.0(139)
Not so good	59.4	15.6	12.5	12.5	100.0(96)
Don't know and other	12.3	4.9	0	82.8	100.0(81)
Average	52.0	12.9	5.5	29.6	100.0(456)

$p < 0.005$

toward Japan, meaning that even the anti-Japanese workers can be very productive.

To summarize the findings for the previous two sections, people who do not gain much satisfaction from their work tend to be anti-Japanese, and these anti-Japanese feelings in turn erode their own identification with the Japanese companies where they work. It should be noted, however, that these anti-Japanese feelings do not necessarily make them any less productive. It should also be added that this is the process at work among core workers but that these core workers are in the minority.

By contrast, most of the rank-and-file workers who derive a feeling of satisfaction from their work are favorably inclined toward Japan and identify strongly with their Japanese companies. However, the ordinary worker's pro-Japanese feelings do not necessarily make her any more productive.

Because the anti-Japanese feelings engendered in the core workers as a result of working for a Japanese company do not lower their productivity, it might be said that the productivity-oriented Japanese company could ignore these anti-Japanese feelings and get on with its primary task of improving production. Yet in terms of Japan's relations with Third World countries in general, it may be expected that anti-Japanese feelings will become stronger and more widespread the more Japanese companies invest in these countries, especially since these core workers hold leadership positions within their local societies. This is clearly an issue that Japanese companies cannot afford to ignore.

Chapter 8
Conclusion

Is Japanese Management Transplantable?

With what we have seen so far, what can we conclude about the transplantability or non-transplantability of Japanese management into other cultures? There remain strong suspicions about the transplantability of Japanese management, and in most cases this takes what might be called the cultural approach. Japanese management was born and bred in a climate of Japanese culture and Japanese values, the skeptics argue, and thus it cannot be easily transplanted into another cultural climate.

Yet most Japanese seem convinced that Japanese management can be transplanted, and they are strong proponents of Japanese management. Odaka refers to this as the nationalistic advocacy of Japanese management. As he explains it, "Triumphant at the praise received, Japanese managers, commentators, and academics have been glorifying the myth and displaying a home-town pride in Japanese management, relentlessly boasting of its good aspects and defending it against all criticism .... Seeing the trend that is occurring in Japan today — the conversion of people to a myth reimported from abroad, and the spread of an attitude of nationalistic glorification and vindication derived from this myth — I cannot help but recall the intellectual climate which prevailed in the years just before World War II when fascism dominated."[1]

Odaka says that Japanese were glad to embrace the myth of Japanese management because (i) it was a myth fostered abroad and thus drew considerable interest by its mere reimportation and (ii) that the Japanese people had an inferiority complex in their relations with the Euro-American nations.[2] In Chapter 1, I have cited some of the fervent advocacy of Japanese management overseas by way of indicating the enthusiasm with which Japanese management is embraced overseas.

On Odaka's second suggestion, that of a Japanese inferiority complex, the following items deserve mention. In the process of modernization, Japan adopted the Euro-American nations as its model, and there was a strong strain of disregard toward the Third World. And when Japan succeeded in approximating Euro-American social and economic institutions, it took it upon itself to tutor these Third World countries.

Thus this fulsome praise from the Euro-American nations made for an easy sense of equality with or even superiority to the West, and this was manifested even more strongly in attitudes toward the Third World countries. As a result, it was easy for Japanese to become ever more convinced about the possibility of transplanting Japanese management worldwide.

From this, there is one conclusion that may be clearly drawn from the data presented in this work. If it is possible to overcome the three non-universal aspects of distinctively Japanese groupism, as indicated in Chapters 2 and 6, it should be possible to transplant Japanese management to other cultural contexts. The first of these three non-universal aspects is the subservience of lower to higher within the hierarchy and the oppression of talent as rationalized in excessive status-consciousness, the second the over-identification with the group, and the third the group-oriented exclusionism and egocentricism. Because these three non-universal aspects are not inherent parts of groupism but are simply reflections of the historic accidents of Japanese society, it is felt that it should be possible to overcome them.

In fact, as seen in Chapters 4 and 5, when Japanese management is transplanted to another society, there are astonishing improvements achieved in both productivity and the humanization of work. The humanization of work will be considered in more detail in the next section, but it should be remembered that there were considerable differences in worker productivity-awareness at the Japanese company that did take Japanese management with it to the United States and the Japanese company that did not. The same phenomenon is seen in the case of Japanese companies practicing Japanese management in Thailand, as both the general workers and the core workers demonstrate an awareness of the need to improve productivity. However, it should be noted that the Thai core workers feel constrained by the non-universal aspects of Japanese management and are critical of Japanese management itself.

If the non-universal aspects of Japanese management can be overcome, Japanese management can be transplanted and major improvements in productivity can be achieved as a result. This means that Japanese management is capable of responding to the American reindustrialization expectations noted in Chapter 1. However, as seen in the next section, there is considerable doubt about whether or not Japanese management will be able to fulfill American expectations for more humanized work.

Japanese Management and Work

What implications does Japanese management have for the humaniza-tion of work? Can Japanese management contribute to improving the quality of work life (QWL) as advocated in the Euro-American countries? These are the questions that this section will attempt to answer.

To review the results of the analysis in Chapter 3, although Japanese workers have a very low level of job satisfaction, they work very hard to raise productivity. It is groupism, sustained by Japanese management, that makes it possible for these contradictory attitudes to co-exist. This means that, having become productivity-oriented, Japanese now emphasize improved productivity over the humanization of work, and this is made possible by groupism.

The overwhelming strength of Japanese management and the resultant friction with the other industrialized countries result basically from the productivity improvements achieved by neglecting the humanization of work. In this sense, it might be said that Japanese management is indeed a form of unfair competition as its critics charge.

Japanese management is very different in other cultural contexts. As seen in Chapter 4's discussion of Japanese companies in the United States, there was more job satisfaction at the Japanese company that practiced Japanese management than at the Japanese company that did not practice Japanese management. This means that the acceptance of Japanese manage-ment brought about a humanization of work and suggests that Japanese management as practiced there is still at the employee welfarism stage. The same was true of the case of ordinary workers at Japanese companies in Thailand, as seen in Chapter 5. There was much more job satisfaction among ordinary Thai workers at Japanese companies.

However, a considerable number of the workers in the United States felt that the Japanese company paid less than other companies, and there was considerable dissatisfaction with the welfare benefits in Thailand. These results indicate that there is strong dissatisfaction with the Japanese company in terms of such hygiene factors as wages and welfare benefits.

Trying to assess future trends from these results, it seems very likely that, if Japanese companies become ever more oriented toward improving productivity, the workers' dissatisfaction will spread from simple hygiene factors to motivational factors and that overseas workers will soon develop the same attitude patterns that Japanese workers have. In fact, this pattern is already evident among Thai core workers, although the reasons for their dissatisfaction are somewhat different.

This seems to indicate a kind of limitation to Japanese management in the humanization of work. Under Maslow's hierarchy of human needs, groupism can be indicative of the need for belonging and love and the need for esteem, but it cannot suffice to satisfy the need for self-actualization. Unless strictly defined and delineated, groupism cannot be an objective for labor.

Thus in judging Japanese management, it is possible to divide the motivational factors into the two levels of groupism and self-actualization. And because groupism can be such a strong motivational factor, it is possible with adroit manipulation of groupism to get people to continue with their work and even to improve productivity even in the face of dissatisfaction on the self-actualization level.

As seen in Chapter 2, Japan has generally passed through the stage of corporate welfarism and entered the new stage of productivity-improvement. Thus it is very likely that Japanese companies operating in other cultures attempting to transplant Japanese management will develop a pattern of seeking productivity through manipulating the workers with groupism. Even non-Japanese companies may develop along the same lines when their primary reason for introducting Japanese management is to raise productivity.

However, this is not a problem inherent or distinctive to Japanese management. Large-scale factory production as symbolized by the conveyer belt and assembly line are negating the workers's own decision-making powers and transforming the worker into a subsidiary part of the production process to raise productivity. Thus so long as factory production exists, it will be very difficult to achieve self-actualization in work under any system, whether it is Japanese management, QWL, or some new expedient. It is the factory system itself that is the real problem in humanizing work.

Of course, this is not to imply that Japanese management is problem-free or that its problems are not important. Japanese management is guilty of spreading the illusion worldwide that it is possible to achieve real improvement in the quality of work with groupism. Given the situation currently prevailing in our industrial societies, it is most important that we recognize the social function that this fiction has served.

Notes

1 Kunio Odaka, *Japanese Management: A Forward-looking Analysis*, Asian Productivity Organization, Tokyo, 1986, pp. 9-10.

2 *Ibid.*, p. 9.

Appendix

Methodology

Survey of Japanese and American Autoworkers

This survey was conducted of Midwestern factory workers employed by American Motors, America's fourth-largest automaker, at its Kenosha plant and workers employed in Japan by Nissan Motor, Japan's number-two automaker, at its Zama plant. The American Motors plant is situated about an hour by car from two major cities, and the factory dominates the small town where it is located.

The questionnaire was designed on the assumption of self-entry and consisted of printed questionnaires and answer cards with the same questions and answer possibilities in English and Japanese. The survey was conducted at American Motors between November 25 and December 4, 1980, and at Nissan Motor between March 6 and March 11, 1981. The sample was selected from the total pool of workers at both plants (including foremen). At American Motors, the universe was 6,620 persons, and at Nissan Motor it was 3,915. After stratifying the workers by workplace and rank so as to ensure that the sample was representative, 200 workers were randomly selected at American Motors and 209 at Nissan. As such, the samples represented 3.0 percent of the total population at American Motors and 5.3 percent of the population at Nissan Motor. The questionnaire, answer sheet, and a return envelope were given to each respondent, and each respondent was asked to answer the questions at home and then to bring the answer sheets back sealed in the envelope. The number of valid responses was 196 at American Motors and 203 at Nissan Motor, meaning that the response rates were, respectively, 98.0 percent and 97.1 percent. Both of these are very high response rates.

Survey of Workers at Japanese Firms in the United States

From among the Japanese companies that had been operating in the United States for five years or longer and were established within their communities, two companies were chosen: one large (in terms of number of employees) and one small. Chosen as the large company, Sony is located in the suburbs of one of the ten largest cities in the West coast in the United States, and there are ample opportunities for employment in this city besides the Sony plant. Chosen as the small company, Kikkoman is located in a Midwestern rural area with no other factories to speak of in the immediate vicinity.

The questionnaire was designed on the assumption of self-entry and consisted of printed questionnaires and answer cards with the same questions and answer possibilities in English. The survey was conducted at Sony from November 14 to November 16, 1978, and at Kikkoman from November 8 to November 10, 1978. The survey was conducted with the voluntary participation of respondents outside of working hours.

The response rate at Sony, where the population was restricted to workers (including foremen) in non-management positions was only 41 out of approximately 800 for a very low 8 percent, but at Kikkoman it was 46 out of a possible 61 for a much more respectable 75 percent.

Survey of Workers at Japanese Firms in Thailand

Japanese companies as defined for the purposes of this survey includes all companies in which there is even minor Japanese equity participation. The survey population was selected in double-random process, the companies first chosen at random and then the survey population chosen at random from among the workers at each company. The total employed population working at Japanese manufacturing concerns in Thailand employing 200 or more persons as listed in the 1974 edition of *Kaigai Shinshutu Kigyo Soran* [Directory to Japanese companies overseas] published by Toyo Keizai Shinpo-sha was taken as the statistical universe, these companies were then divided by industry (textiles, glass, chemicals, automobiles, electrical equipment, foodstuffs, and others) and by size (2,000 or more, 1,000 to 1,999, 500 to 999, and 200 to 499 employees), and then ten company groups were selected so as to be proportionally representative of all 39,924 persons working at these Japanese companies in Thailand. Each group consisted of three companies. This method was adopted so that it would be possible to select another company out of the same group should one of the companies chosen decide not to cooperate with the survey. The actual selection of respondents was to select 60 persons from each company below the level of section chief or equivalent managerial position.

In the end, the cooperation was obtained from eight companies and a total of 456 employees, which was 76 percent of the originally planned 600. As such, this represented 1.14 percent of the total population. The actual survey itself was conducted by gathering all of the respondents from a given company in one room and then having them fill out the questionnaire with supplemental instruction and guidance from an experienced interviewer. The survey was conducted from August 30 to September 10, 1975.

Survey of Japanese Joint-venture Partners in Thailand

This survey was conducted of all of the chief executives of Thai companies having joint ventures with Japanese companies in manufacturing in Thailand. The questionnaires were distributed at the end of October 1979 and the results collected in early December 1979. As before, Japanese companies as defined here includes all companies with even minor Japanese equity participation. For the survey itself, respondents were asked to check the appropriate response on preprinted answer cards in Thai. The distribution of questionnaires was handled by having the Japan Overseas Enterprises Association's Bangkok Consulting Office distribute questionnaires to the Japanese companies and having the Japanese companies give them directly to their Thai partners. Responses were mailed directly to the Japan Overseas Enterprises Association's Bangkok Consulting Office. To ensure better compliance, the responses were anonymous and every effort was made to protect the respondent company's identity.

There are 124 Japanese manufacturing firms in Thailand. Of these, two have no Thai partners, leaving a total of 122 possible subject companies for this survey. Because 51 completed answer sheets were received, the response rate was thus 42 percent, which is very high for a survey of this kind.

Group Discussions with Thai Workers and Executives

Four discussion groups were formed, one each for intellectuals, workers, young bureaucrats, and executives, and each discussion group met separately. Each group was shown a pre-printed sheet similar to that in Table A-1 (showing only the discussion subjects for workers and executives) to guide the discussion. Each group included five or six Thai citizens plus one moderator who moderated all of the group discussions. There were no Japanese present. The discussions were held for about two hours each on June 20, 1975, for the executives' group and on July 2, 1975, for the workers. The discussions were recorded, and translated into English by the moderator. Although the names and identities of discussion participants were given in the main text itself, a summary listing is given in Table A-2 for reference.

Table A-1. Focus Group Discussion Topics

	Workers	Executives
1	If you were going to change jobs and there were three companies for you to choose from — a Japanese company, a Thai company, and an American company — which one would you want to work for and why?	Do you feel that, as a joint venture partner, Japanese companies are good partners? What are their merits? What kind of problems and disadvantages does a Japanese company have as a partner?
2	According to the results of a television survey of a year ago, Japanese were considered selfish and unkind. What do you think of these findings? Conversely, what are some typical Japanese traits which you admire?	In Japan-Thai joint ventures, it's usually been the Thai side handling sales and the Japanese side handling production. Do you see this pattern continuing? What do you think should happen?
3	Has the Thai workers lifestyle improved compared with 10 years ago? What are some reasons for this? Have Thai workers been exploited by foreign capitalized companies?	To what extent is the Thai business community dominated by people of Chinese descent? Have the Thai-Chinese fully integrated into Thai society? (Do you consider yourself a Thai citizen?)
4	Please describe the type of boss you would like to work for. Is it someone who takes care of you even outside of work? What do you think of Japanese superiors?	

Table A-2. Focus Group Members

A. Workers

Name	Ethnic background	Sex	Age	Marital status	Education	Type of company worked for	Note
Virat	Thai	M	25-30	Married	Secondary	Home appliances	
Vichai	Chinese	M	35-40	Married	Secondary	Cosmetics	
Aroon	Chinese	M	30-35	Married	Vocational	Cosmetics	
Warin	Chinese	M	25-30	Single	Technical college	Chemicals	Has worked for Japanese company
Prasert	Thai	M	25-30	Married	Secondary	Home appliances	Japanese company
Sompong	Chinese	M	25-30	Single	College	Chemicals	

Table A-2. (Continued)

B. Executives

Name	Ethnic background	Sex	Age	Marital status	Education	Type of company worked for	Note
Boonyasitt	Chinese	M	35-40	Married	Secondary	Investment company	Considerable dealings with Japanese companies
Sarinthron	Chinese	F	30-35	Single	University (accounting)	Finance and insurance	
Chomchai	Thai	M	30-35	Married	University	Textile manufacture	Joint venture with Japanese company
Maitree	Thai	M	35-40	Married	University (engineering)	Home appliances	
Suthep	Chinese	M	30-35	Married	University	Consumer goods	

Related Papers By The Same Author

Changing Pattern of Japanese Attitudes toward Work: A consequence of Recent High Economic Growth, English Pamphlet Series, No. 67, Institute of Population Problems, Tokyo, 1969.

"Kaigai Toshi no Shakaigakuteki Kenkyu" [Sociological study of overseas investment], in *Nihon Kigyo no Kaigai Katsudo wo Meguru Shomondai no Kenkyu* [Study of issues in overseas activity by Japanese companies], 1976 (all in Japanese).

"Beikokujin Rodosha to Nihonteki Rodo Kanri" [American workers and Japanese-style labor management] in *Nihon no Taibei Chokusetu Toshi ni Kansuru Kenkyu* [Studies on Japanese direct investment in the United States], 1979 (all in Japanese).

"Beikokujin Rodosha no Ishiki" [American workers' attitudes], in *Nihon Kigyo in USA* [Japanese companies in the United States], edited by Toshio Shishido and Nikko Research Center, Toyo Keizai Shinpo-sha, Tokyo, 1980 (all in Japanese).

ASEAN Shokoku ni okeru Nikkei Kigyo no Genchi Koken Jokyo ni Kansuru Chosa Kenkyu [Survey of Japanese companies' contribution to local community in ASEAN countries], Japan Overseas Enterprises Association, 1980 (in Japanese).

"Nihonteki Keiei no Fuhensei" [The universality of Japanese-style management] in *Wagakuni Sangyo no Kyoryoku ni yoru Beikoku Sangyo no Kasseika* [Revitalizing American industry with Japanese industrial cooperation],Nikko Research Center, 1981 (all in Japanese).